ANCIENT
INTUITION

Ignite the Spark of Awareness

Already Within You

Debra May Macleod

The author is not engaged in rendering professional advice or services to the individual reader. The ideas and strategies presented herein are for general informational purposes only. Only the reader can judge the suitability of this book's content to his/her life. Part of this book explains the author's use of candles in a spiritual/ritual capacity: any descriptions or instructions are based solely on the author's practices and are for general informational purposes only. Should the reader choose to engage in any flame or candle-burning rituals, he or she must take appropriate fire-safe precautions and use his or her own judgment (i.e. burn in fire-safe receptacles, never leave a flame unattended, have a means of extinguishment nearby, etc.). A candle is an open flame and must be treated as such. The author will not be held liable for any act or omission allegedly arising, directly or indirectly, from the use or misuse of this book.

Cover photo: Ring of fire © Christine Kuehnel Shutterstock.com

Ebook formatting by Maureen Cutajar.

Interior illustrations:
Monochrome retro starburst © Ezepov Dmitry. Shutterstock.com ID:254946016
Primitive figures cave painting © De-V. Shutterstock.com ID:77643556
Background in Greek style. © Thumbelina. Shutterstock.com ID:330230057
Illustration Temple of Vesta. Public Domain. From author's collection.
Background in Greek style. © Thumbelina. Shutterstock.com ID:174105890
Wikimedia Commons, Family Tree of the Human Race, ca. 1877, Ernest Haeckel.
Flat Honey Bee in Honeycomb © Crystal Eye Studio
Shutterstock.com ID:289671422
Background in Greek style. © Thumbelina. Shutterstock.com ID:141792163
Background in Greek style. © Thumbelina. Shutterstock.com ID:136225136
Background in Greek style. © Thumbelina. Shutterstock.com ID:246879058
The Greek near a cup with fire. © Thumbelina. Shutterstock.com ID:126191315
Background in Greek style. © Thumbelina. Shutterstock.com ID:141792154
Planetary sign for Vesta 4. Public Domain. Wikimedia Commons.
Letter V logo © Steinar Image ID # 206140168 Provided by Shutterstock.com

TABLE OF CONTENTS

Foreword:
WHAT IS ANCIENT INTUITION?

Why do I feel so nervous about getting on this airplane?
How come I don't believe what this person is telling me?
I know I should turn here. I feel drawn to this place...
Something isn't right. I need to call home.
What made me feel drawn to this book?
I feel like the universe is trying to tell me something...
I know my life is changing. How can I understand what's happening?

Most of us know what intuition is – it's that phenomenon of the mind whereby we "just know" something without having or needing evidence. It's a mix of thought, idea and feeling. You might describe it as a gut feeling or your little voice. This is how the dictionary describes it:

Simple Definition of INTUITION (Merriam-Webster)

1 : a natural ability or power that makes it possible to know something without any proof or evidence: a feeling that guides a person to act in a certain way without fully understanding why
2 : something that is known or understood without evidence

This definition is likely similar to your own. Indeed, tapping into one's intuition is something that almost all humans inherently recognize and have experienced. Some of us even rely on it and there's no doubt that enhancing intuition can lead to a more fulfilling and fascinating life.

But how do we tap into our intuition so that we can get more out of life? How do we learn to master it?

The weight of current literature on intuition speaks of a New Age or a "dawning age" of intuition, one where humankind is progressing and evolving into intuitive beings. The idea is that this progression is an entirely new concept, an unchartered journey of the soul as humans develop their intuitive selves and tune into a higher "frequency" of being.

I don't get this. To me, this sounds like we're all marching toward some New Age plateau and, when we get there, we're all going to magically morph into futuristic beings of pure light or energy like characters in a *Star Trek* episode. It sounds like our goal is to evolve into a new and improved species of *Homo sapiens*. *Homo superiens*, maybe?

Ancient Intuition challenges the supposition that intuition is new or advanced. It isn't. In fact, intuition is old and fundamental. Intuition is *ancient*. It is as ancient as the first molecule, the first star, the first breath, the first thought, the first fire. And it waited eons for us as a species – and for you as an individual – to bring it to life as a sixth sense.

Through the ages, we have interpreted our intuition in different ways: from pre-history and proto-history to the Classical Age, through the Dark Ages, to the Renaissance and finally to the Modern or Digital Age.

Yet the truth remains: intuition is ancient and no matter how many "ages" we go through, the purest spark of intuition can only be ignited by going back in time: back to the beginning of the universe, back to the beginning of who we are as a species. *Back to ancient you.* And this little book – this little time machine in your hands – can help you do that.

PART I

PRE-HISTORY

&

PROTO-HISTORY

PERCEPTION

A Long Time Ago:
A Spark of Insight

A long time ago, perhaps a million or more years ago, a group of pre-*Homo sapiens* hominids sat huddled together on a chilly, stormy night when – out of the cloudy black abyss above them – a bolt of electric light slammed into a nearby tall tree with a deafening boom.

Whoosh! The tree erupted into flames. The ground around the tree sizzled as red embers poked through the burned grass.

Frightened, the group jumped to its feet to rush into the safety of their cave. All but one, that is. One of the group stood rigid, more fascinated than afraid, and stared at the burning tree.

The fire's light reflected in her eyes while the snap of its flames echoed in her ears. Its heat energy radiated toward her, warming her flesh and permeating her being. Despite the fearful heat and the snapping wood, she took a step closer.

A large beehive had fallen out of the tree and a thick honeycomb was melting into the ground. Even through the smoke of the fire, she could smell the sweet fragrance of honey and burning beeswax.

She had a thought...no, an idea. No, a feeling. No, something else. Not just a thought or an idea or a feeling...somehow it was all of those things, and more.

It was intuition. This *meant* something.

The next day, the heat of the summer sun once again beat down on the group. Some busied themselves with collecting berries while others tended to the young. A few struggled to skin an animal the chief hunter had killed.

But the curious old female sat on a large stone by herself, seemingly mesmerized by the black charred ground that surrounded the base of the scorched tree. Although the fire had long since gone out, dots of red embers still smoldered beneath the singed black grass.

The female experienced it again – the thought-idea-feeling. And then she just knew what to do.

She got up from her large stone and collected a handful of dry grass from beneath some nearby bushes. Gently, she placed the dry grass on the smoldering embers.

The fire crackled back to life. It began to spread out, consuming the dry grass she had placed on top of it. Soon, however, it encountered the barrier of a smooth stone and faltered, threatening to go out.

The female's thought-idea-feeling grew stronger.

If I place more stones around the fire, and if I keep placing more grass on top of the fire, it will continue to burn in the area I want it to. I can control it.

So she did. She created a circle of stones. She kept placing grass on top of the fire. And it worked. The fire kept going, just like she knew it would.

She heard a shout at her shoulder. One of the younger males was pointing to her, to the fire, and back to her. He called the rest of the group and they stared wide-eyed at the fire and the female.

The chief hunter appeared. His eyes were wide. He waved at the female. *Keep doing that.*

The old female pushed the young male at her shoulder, urging him to collect more dry grass from the field. He did. The fire smoked and crackled.

But the female wasn't satisfied. She looked up at the scorched, dead tree and remembered how the flames had raged along its branches. She remembered how the wood had burned long, strong and hot. It didn't smoke as much as the grass, either. She called upon the thought-idea-feeling.

And then she just knew what to do. She stepped away from the fire and returned a moment later with branches which she laid over the low fire.

Whoosh! The fire was strong now and it required less work to keep it going. The group jumped and shouted and laughed, and even the chief hunter laughed and was pleased.

Over the next week or so, the female tended to the fire non-stop. She taught some of the other females, including her female offspring, how to keep the fire going so that they could tend it while she slept.

She taught them which wood burned the best and how to lay it crisscross over the flames so the fire could breathe. She taught them how to contain the fire within the circle of stones.

Soon, the group began to spend more time outside the cave, especially at night. The predators that had formerly circled the camp under the cover of dark, causing terror and confusion by hunting them at night, seemed afraid of the fire and had stopped coming so close.

They sat by the fire and felt its heat warm their bodies in the cool night air. They stared at the dancing flames, captivated by their movement and beauty and grace.

Some members of the group began to dance like the flames and hold up their arms to the starry sky. The red embers that glowed through the black ash of the fire seemed strikingly similar to the silver embers that glowed through black canopy of the night sky.

Every time a red spark snapped and flew out of the fire, they imagined it flying up into the firmament above. Did the sparks turn into stars?

They felt amazed by the mysterious power of the fire – it must *mean* something! – and the first feelings of spiritual reverence stirred in the human soul.

But then it rained and the fire went out.

The group quickly went back to their old ways, huddling for warmth and scanning the trees and darkness for the predators that were once again closing in. As soon as dark fell, they couched in their cave. They missed the fire.

The curious old female missed it most of all. The thought-idea-feeling that she had first experienced on the night of the thunderbolt and the tree fire would not leave her.

She knew what she needed to do. She needed to find a way to start the fire herself. It was no good to rely on thunderbolts from the sky. It was no good to rely on smoldering embers on the ground. She had to control the fire.

She withdrew and sat alone behind the cave for days. Her offspring brought her food and water but she would not eat or drink anything.

The chief hunter ordered her to return; however, she refused even him and he conceded. She had discovered the fire and, even though it no longer burned, it was a remarkable feat that had increased her status in the group.

It was here, behind the cave, that the group's tool-makers chipped, hammered and shaped both bone and stone into tools and weapons.

The female watched them closely. She watched a stone hit another stone and – what was that? – a spark, no different than the ones that flew from the fire!

The thought-idea-feeling was overwhelming now. *A spark can do the same thing as a thunderbolt!*

Breathing hard, she ran up to the tool-maker and took the sparking stones from his hands. He thought about hitting her but he knew the chief hunter would beat him so he didn't.

She ran to the spot where the fire had burned, and chased everyone way, even her own offspring. She sat on the ground for hours with her back turned to them.

All they could see were her arms moving and all they could hear was the tapping and scraping sounds of the stones in her hands.

What was she doing?

And then finally, she stood up. She took a step back and – to the shock and awe of everyone – she pointed at the ground.

She had started a fire herself.

From that day on, they called her Firestarter.

Soon, fire became the focus of the group's life and activities, both day and night. They discovered that it offered even more than warmth from the cold, safety from predators and light in the darkness.

A clumsy child dropped his portion of the kill into the fire and his father pulled the meat out with a stick. He made the child eat it as punishment; however, the smell enticed them all and soon everyone was throwing their portion in the fire and eating it. Cooked.

It tasted wonderful.

The fire had transformed them and their way of life. It had illuminated something within them, and they all knew who was responsible for it.

Even though she was a female years past her fertility, even though her mate was long-dead and no longer there to protect her or make sure she got a share of the kill, Firestarter had suddenly become one the group's most respected and important members. She had all the food she wanted.

She taught other females, including her three daughters, how to start fire and keep it going. She was always learning more and passing on what she learned.

Together, they found that certain sounds and movements made the fire start faster or burn stronger, so they remembered these sounds and movements and began to perform them every time they started a fire.

These actions – these rituals – seemed to please the spirit of the fire, so they took great care to reproduce them perfectly every time.

One night, the group was sleeping peacefully around the fire inside their warm cave when Firestarter's thought-idea-feeling woke her in a panic.

Even though she was very old and it hurt to move, she crept to the chief hunter and shook him violently.

He woke with an angry start and stared at her – she was pointing beyond the entrance of the cave, into the dark beyond.

The chief hunter looked into the darkness but saw nothing. He strained his ears, but heard nothing. He wanted to push her away and go back to sleep, but the look in her eyes made him think twice. He was learning not to ignore Firestarter's secret awareness of things.

He gathered his strongest hunters and they took their weapons into the dark beyond the fire-lit cave.

Shouts and screams followed. Fear, surprise, agony. The group huddled around the fire, waiting for their fate.

But soon, the chief hunter and his fighters returned. They made excited sounds in front of Firestarter and moved in a circle around her, touching her legs and feet.

The next morning, when the group exited the cave, they found ten dead bodies – a rival group on a raid – piled on top of each other.

Time went on. More and more the group worked as one, seeming to just know what needed to be done. The fire had sparked a certain curiosity in all of them and they began to be aware of their world in a new way.

If they could control fire, why not the water? The trees? The animals? The world?

As Firestarter grew even older and more frail, the group twisted branches into shapes and gave them to her as gifts. The chief hunter gave her the second cut of his kills, second only to his own.

But then one morning they awoke to find her stiff and unmoving in the tall grasses behind the cave. They were about to leave her body there, but then the thought-idea-feeling came to Firestarter's oldest daughter.

She just knew what to do next. She showed the others how to start a larger and very special fire – a holy fire – by placing the finest stones they could find in a circle around it.

They set Firestarter's body upon it and added the best wood until the flames the curious old female loved so much consumed her body in the same way they consumed the grass and wood.

When the fire went out, Firestarter's oldest daughter collected her bones. She spread the wet ashes of her mother's remains on her cheeks and her sisters' cheeks, and some members of the group had the thought-idea-feeling that the sisters' grief was even greater than their own.

They gave the sisters their portions of the kill and sat for long periods beside them in silence, even on those days that were best for splashing in the river or looking for mates.

Then one night, when they were all sitting by the fire, Firestarter's oldest daughter held out one of her mother's white bones to the group.

As a spark snapped out of the fire and flew up to become a star in the night sky, she pointed the bone toward the stars. A strange sound came out of her throat.

They all had a thought-idea-feeling. It was a new but comforting one, and somehow they just knew it was true. *Firestarter was like a spark, and she was sparkling above them.*

And religion was born from death.

The months went on. One morning, Firestarter's oldest daughter was tending to the fire when she spotted someone hiding in the trees and staring at her with wide eyes.

She recognized him as a young scout from a neighboring group, a peaceful group that sometimes went to the same river as her group.

She waved him over to the fire and he jumped up and down around it, running away when a spark popped out but then quickly coming back. She showed him how the circle of stones kept the fire in control.

She gave him a cooked piece of meat. His mouth exploded with taste and he felt a strangely pleasant warmth spread throughout his stomach.

He looked around the group's grassy home. There were three piles of large kills. How could one group be such good hunters? How could they catch so many animals? There were more kills than one group could even eat!

The chief hunter saw the young male standing by the fire with Firestarter's daughter. He saw the young male studying the piles of kills and the fire.

An idea came to him.

He had the idea to give the young male a gift. He sensed this gift would please the other group's chief hunter.

So he gave Firestarter's daughter as a mate to the young male. As the young female left to join her new group, the chief hunter instructed her to take two sparking stones with her.

Not long after that, the neighboring group's chief hunter came with gifts of his own: tools and weapons that his tool-makers had invented.

These tools and weapons were remarkable and better than anything Firestarter's chief hunter had seen.

The two chief hunters sat by the fire all night, eating cooked meat and watching the sparks fly away. They inspected each other's tools and weapons for hours.

As they did, they had the thought-idea-feeling that it was good they were together in this way. They sensed that their mates and offspring would be safer if they could combine their knowledge and abilities.

They sensed that their combined warriors would be able to fight off any invasions from the violent groups that surrounded them. They would also be better able to fight off their animal predators.

They sensed that their combined tool-makers would be able to create even better tools and weapons for protection and hunting.

They sensed that their combined hunters would be able to kill even more animals. They would not need to feel hunger again.

And then there were the females. There would be more of them, and different ones, too. That meant more offspring. That meant more females that could do things like make fire.

As the night wore on and they developed these ideas by the fire, Firestarter's daughters performed the ritual sounds and movements that their mother had taught them, the ones that they knew best pleased the spirit of the fire.

* * * * * *

It is true that pre-historic fire worship of the kind depicted here was the first form of religion known to humankind, or to what would eventually become humankind.

The desire to control and honor fire was intuitive in nature. It was planted in humanity during the infancy of our species, and it allowed us to grow into what we are today.

We built our homes, societies, social structures and cultures around fire. We began to intuitively grasp the grand scope of our intelligence and our unlimited potential around fire. No wonder we have always seen it as sacred.

As you will see as you move through this book, other discoveries – from mathematics to morality – were also intuitive in nature and essential for our growth as a species.

So too were the practical aspects of intuition, the ones that allow us to avoid danger and make the right decisions in life, especially when we don't have all the facts.

That gut feeling. That little voice. The skill to utilize the principles of the law of attraction and mind over matter to our advantage. The insight and skill to recognize coincidence for what it really is. And so on.

Yet the most compelling and intuitive desire of all is to know ourselves on a personal level.

We long for the awareness – and the ability – to both understand and master our true potential as an individual apart from the group.

The universe planted this desire, these seeds of intuition, in humanity at the dawn of our awakening. You already harbor that seed of ancient intuition within you. It's there, even if it is dormant.

Once you learn to give it life and master it, you can finally grow into the person you want to be. You can finally grow into the person you were meant to be.

Intuition is the universe speaking to you. It's the most primal element of your being calling out to you.

You're no different than Firestarter. She heard the call as a deafening thunderbolt. How do you hear it?

PROMETHEUS: FIRE & AWARENESS

The rituals performed around the fires of our distant hominid ancestors – like Firestarter and her group– continued from pre-history (the time before written records) throughout the centuries to proto-history (the time when humans began to write down their stories and history).

This "religion of fire" eventually spread and evolved into the various myths, legends and histories of many different cultures as humankind flourished and moved upon the Earth. Indeed, this is still evident in the 21st century. Fire – including candle-burning – remains a fundamental part of spiritual and religious expression in almost every culture.

The story of Prometheus is one of the first stories in our Western culture where the idea of intuition is explored and exalted. And it shouldn't come as a surprise that fire is the element used to symbolize this intuition.

Ancient Greek poets writing as far back as 1100 BCE – Homer, followed by Hesiod and others -- first tell us the story of Prometheus. There are many variations and hybrid versions, but essentially it goes something like this.

Prometheus is the son of a Titan who dares to challenge the omnipotence of Zeus, the chief god of the twelve Olympian gods and goddesses. In an act of defiance to Zeus and friendship to humankind, Prometheus gives the "gift of fire" to early humans. That is, he teaches someone very like our Firestarter how to start and control fire.

This discovery changes everything. Humans are no longer slaves to the mysteries and whims of the gods. For by learning to control fire, they have illuminated their own intuition. They have illuminated what they truly are and what they can become. Fire symbolizes awareness, intelligence and self-determination.

Of course, Zeus is less than pleased. In fact, he's downright grumpy and vengeful about the whole thing. After all, it is much better for a god to keep humans in the dark.

To punish Prometheus for revealing this secret to humankind, Zeus chains him to a rock on a mountainside. Every day, an eagle – Zeus's symbolic animal – flies to Prometheus and eats his liver. Every night, Prometheus is re-born so his torment can continue the following day.

Yikes.

But don't worry. As luck would have it, the hero Hercules unchains Prometheus during one of his celebrated twelve labors. So all's well that ends well, I suppose.

Yet here's an interesting thing about Zeus: despite his general lack of humor about the whole thing, he doesn't take fire away from humankind.

Why not? Who knows. Perhaps even the greatest of the gods knew that human intuition, once ignited, can't be snuffed out again.

And you know it, too.

Think back. Have there not been times in your life when your intuition just wouldn't leave you alone? Have there not been times when that "little voice" inside you kept nagging you to "do this" or "stop doing that"?

This book talks a lot about human history. But you have a history, too. Your past history is your own personal antiquity. Just as an archaeologist excavates the ground to expose the truth and gain awareness of things not seen on the surface, so too must you excavate your own life to expose and gain awareness of your own truth.

Back to that "little voice" of yours. What was it trying to tell you? Did you listen to it? Why or why not? What happened when you followed it? Ignored it?

Your little voice might have been telling you something about a relationship you were in. Indeed, this is a common area where intuition speaks to us. After all, it knows how deeply we can be loved – or hurt – by an intimate partner. Yet whether or not we listen to our intuition is another matter.

As a couples' mediator, I've heard countless clients in unhappy relationships say, "I just knew it would never change. I should have listened to myself sooner."

So why didn't they listen to themselves? Well, for any number of reasons. Perhaps they believed they had invested too many years in the relationship to just "give up." Perhaps they didn't have the resources to get out or believed their children were better off if they stayed.

Or perhaps they let other voices – those desperate voices of hopelessness or false hope, of fear, of regret or confusion – drown out the softer voice of their intuition.

It will get better if I just give him/her another chance! I know he/she loves me! I'll miss him/her too much. I'm too old, who will want me now? I can't make it on my own. Everyone will think I'm unlovable. I'm afraid to be alone.

Of course, there are many other areas of life where intuition "nags" us to make the right choice for us. In fact, I'd say intuition speaks to us about all aspects of life.

For example, I knew in my first year of law school that I didn't want to be there. All I could think about was how much I missed the fascinating and remarkably *familiar* sense of discovery I felt during my undergraduate studies in Greco-Roman history and the Classics.

I knew that I should have withdrawn from law school and went back to follow my passion. But I didn't. I listened to other voices, particularly the "voice of reason."

You can't withdraw! You've been working your ass off for four years to get into this law school! A legal career will pay better than a career as a professor or curator. Stay the course.

So I did. And it wasn't all bad. I did well, graduated, and started my own mediation practice which gave me the flexibility to balance work, marriage and baby in a way that too few women have the luxury of doing.

I can't say I *regret* the course I took. But there's no doubt a career as a Classics professor or a museum curator would have been a more exciting and natural one for me.

Yet those embers of intuition never go out. They're like the smoldering embers under Firestarter's scorched tree. That little voice keeps nagging us until we finally listen.

Throughout my years as a mediator and relationship author-expert, I kept studying Classical history. I was especially interested in ancient religion. For those of you who have read my previous book *The Vesta Secret*, you'll know why, but I'll bring the rest of you up to speed in a little while.

Suffice it to say, my current life and career are all about Classical history and ancient religion. I'm more immersed in them now than if I'd become a Classics professor or a museum curator.

That's why this book exists. It exists because it is impossible to stamp out the embers of intuition. It is impossible to gag that little voice.

You can try, of course. You might even convince yourself that you've succeeded and that you're good with the way things are. But your intuition won't play along.

That doesn't mean you should regret your past. It's part of your story and your growth. Don't worry if you've missed a shortcut or two and have had to take the long way to get here. It's no matter. You're here now. And you followed your intuition to get here. See? It really does work.

Your ancient intuition knows what it will take for you to be happy and fulfilled in this life. It has absolute awareness and it cannot be silenced. Its embers cannot be stamped out. The universe gave it sacred power and eternal life.

And even Zeus knew better than to mess with that.

ANCIENT INTUITION: THE MASTER TEACHER

The word intuition comes to us from the Latin word intueri. It means to look inside or within, or to understand without the use of reason. In fact, our modern conception and understanding of intuition, as well as the high regard we have for it, comes largely from ancient Greco-Roman culture.

The first written records we have about intuition come to us from these ancient civilizations, including and perhaps especially the Greeks who saw intuition and intelligence as two sides of the same coin. They recognized the necessity, power and ability of human intuition. They refined intuition and they revered it.

Greek masters of philosophy – including Plato and Aristotle who lived and taught in the 4th century BCE – extolled the value of intuition. The latter actually said that "Intuition is the source of scientific knowledge."

Pythagoras, the ancient world's master of mathematics and metaphysics, felt the same and relied upon intuition when formulating his Pythagorean theorem, as well as his theories regarding numbers, logic and truth.

These great thinkers and doers were fascinated by the ability of the human mind to formulate abstract ideas. That is, the ability of the human mind to conceive "something from nothing." And they attributed this ability to intuition.

It's one thing to formulate the idea of clothing, for example. Early humans *felt* cold. They *saw* and *felt* the warm fur pelts of their kills.

Using a combination of ancient intuition and ever-evolving intelligence, they invented the idea of clothing. It's an impressive invention, to be sure.

But it pales in comparison to the intuitive powers needed to formulate a purely abstract or non-sensory mathematical formula or recognize a pattern.

It pales in comparison to the intuitive powers needed to recognize the difference between right and wrong (that is, to moralize) or to ponder the meaning of life.

Nonetheless, the human desire to engage in those abstract pursuits is as strong as the desire to wear warm clothing and control fire.

Which begs the question: Why would we as a species care about such esoteric and enigmatic concepts? Why would we devote so much time and energy to inscrutable questions? Why all the mental gymnastics?

Strictly speaking, humankind can get by without things like philosophy, metaphysics and mathematics.

We don't need them. We can't eat them. We can't wear them. And frankly, they give some of us a killer headache.

Nonetheless, our ancient intuition incessantly nags us. *You are more than this. There is more to life. Ignite your awareness! Decipher the universe! Master yourself! Figure it out, you clever ape!*

According to Plato, humans use abstract ideas to explore, understand and explain both the world around us and the world within us.

And it is intuition that allows us to recognize unreal things as being very real indeed.

For example, a math equation isn't real in the same way that a kitchen table is real. Yet most humans would agree that math is real. We know it helps us explain our world. We know it's real because our intuition tells us that it's real.

This kind of ancient perception – the ability to recognize abstract concepts as reality – was ingrained into us at the dawn of humankind.

You might say that our ancient intuition is the code-breaker we have been given to discover life's secrets. It helps us pull order out of disorder, and to organize what appears to be disorganized. It shows us that what seems to be abstract is in fact wholly intact.

But what does this have to do with you, you might ask?

Well, everything. It has *everything* to do with you because you are made of tangible and intangible things.

You are made of real and unreal things. Flesh and bone: tangible and real. Emotion, ideas and intuition: intangible and unreal.

You also have abilities that are physical and metaphysical. You can physically pick up a pen or cook supper. But you can also metaphysically ponder the nature of your existence and tap into your intuitive abilities to enhance your awareness of the universe and achieve a better life.

Like any master teacher, our ancient intuition is always encouraging us to do better. Many people feel the "push" of intuitive perception that compels them move toward a greater awareness of things.

We are compelled to climb a mountain, only to reach the top and look up at the moon, thinking, "*Ah, you're next.*"

Yet this compulsion is often a dangerous one. The push of intuition is sometimes at odds with "the facts." After all, it's dangerous as hell to rocket to the moon. But we do it anyway.

However, the most courageous – and intuitive – of us recognize that human curiosity is an integral part of intuition. Curiosity – *What's up there? What will happen if I do this?* – is a very special "tone" that our little voice takes when it wants us to explore something further.

That exploration can take place on the moon, but it can also take place in your life, in your relationship, in your career, in your financial situation, in your hobbies or passions, in your creativity, in your location, in your spirituality or self-awareness.

And as you move through subsequent parts of this book – particularly Part III and Part IV which are especially "hands on" – we'll tackle the intuitive exploration of these various aspects of your life in an insightful yet highly practical step-by-step way.

THE ETERNAL FLAME
OF ANCIENT INTUITION

Do you remember the way that Firestarter so carefully placed stones in a circle to encompass her fire? Do you remember how her daughter so reverently placed even finer stones around the first "holy fire" imagined by humans?

Well, that custom evolved until that circle of pre-historic stones embracing a simple fire became a circle of fine marble embracing a sacred hearth within the Temple of Vesta.

Located in the heart of the Roman Forum, this round temple was the first in ancient Rome. Legend has it that it was built to house a sacred fire started by Romulus, Rome's founder, whose intuition told him to build the Eternal City around that very spot. The ruins of this temple still stand today: in fact, they grace the cover of this book.

Vesta, goddess of the home and hearth, is symbolized by fire. The ancient Romans believed she resided in their household fires and beeswax candles. Her presence in their home and hearts made these spaces sacred. To nourish her spirit and bless their home, they sprinkled offerings of salted flour or libations of olive oil, milk or wine into her flame.

Although originally a household spirituality, her worship spread to the public sphere. Her temple was in the very heart of Rome and six Vestal priestesses kept her eternal flame going at all times. It was believed that if Vesta's fire went out, so too would the Roman way of life.

Remember how Firestarter's group worked to preserve their fire? How they toiled to keep it going day and night and perform rituals around it to please the spirit of the fire?

Remember how they intuitively knew that the flame represented something sacred, something essential?

Well, the Romans thought the same way, although their rituals were performed with a lot more pomp and ceremony. Ancient Rome had a "go big or go home" way of doing things.

I mentioned previously that I have long been fascinated with ancient religion. Curiously enough, that fascination started at this very temple.

When I was twenty years old, and before I went to university, I took a solo trip to Italy. Late one chilly March afternoon, I found myself wandering along the Via Sacra, the cobblestone road that runs through the Roman Forum.

On either side of this road, massive columns and stones lay scattered, silent monuments to the grandeur of the past. It's almost as if, centuries ago, Jupiter scooped every temple in his hands, crushed them, and sprinkled them along the road.

As I approached the ruins of the temple, I met an old woman burning an aged beeswax candle near the site of the sacred hearth. Her name was Camilla. And although I didn't realize it at the time, she would ultimately become the most influential person I would ever meet in my life.

It was she who first told me about this ancient fire-based tradition and who explained how the "Flamma" (Latin for Flame) could spark the ancient intuition that every one of us carries within.

That shouldn't come as a surprise. We've already seen how fire sparked the primal intuitive powers of early hominids, such as our Firestarter.

It is only natural that the metaphysical use of fire would continue to evolve, becoming more sophisticated as humankind moved from pre-history to the Classical Age.

In fact, it was during this Classical Age that fire was most widely revered – especially in a formal capacity through elaborate ritual – for its various protective and spiritual aspects, including its ability to ignite intuitive awareness.

For example, the ancients saw meaning in the way fire changes and moves. They saw meaning in the way it is dynamic, yet consistent.

Even as it continues to burn, it transforms to embers and sparks. To light, to sound and to heat. As the wood shifts in the hearth, or the wind catches the flame of a candle, fire adapts and stays alight.

These remarkable qualities showcase why fire is so symbolic of eternity, the universe and the soul. As we go through life, do we not change and adapt, yet remain who we are?

As we move through death, do we not change again, the soul flying out of the body like a spark snapping out a fire?

This parallel is something the ancient Romans and their beloved Vestal priestesses recognized and revered.

They intuitively knew that protecting the eternal flame in its sacred hearth was the same as protecting the soul within the body.

They intuitively knew that protecting the eternal flame protected their eternal city. And they built an elaborate state religion around this intuitive knowledge.

In the process, Firestarter's circle of prehistoric stones around a fledgling fire evolved into the circular Classical temple that housed a sacred and eternal fire.

In the process, the simple sounds and movements Firestarter and her apprentices made to please the spirit of the fire evolved into the elaborate religious rituals the Vestal priestesses performed to please their fiery goddess.

Yet the fundamental perception of fire as a spiritual faculty remained unchanged. So too did the knowledge that fire has the ability to ignite the ancient intuition and awareness already within us.

Illustration of the Temple of Vesta.

THE DARKNESS
& THE LIGHT

For over a thousand years, the Temple of Vesta stood in the Roman Forum. For over a thousand years, the eternal flame burned in its sacred hearth, providing protection and inspiration to Rome, and elaborating upon the tradition of fire worship that began in pre-history with Firestarter.

For over a thousand years, the Classical world thrived. Science, medicine, philosophy, mathematics, astronomy, art and literature took root and sprouted, nourished by the spirit of discovery of the times.

Socially, the ideas of secular law, justice and fairness prevailed and – due in large part to the esteemed status of the Vestal priestesses – early women's rights began to arise.

All of this was fueled by intuition which continued to be recognized across all disciplines, from philosophy to science, as a core aspect of humankind's existence.

Intuition was regarded as a sixth sense. It was simply one more way of perceiving the world, a natural addition to the five senses classified by none other than our intuitive friend Aristotle: sight, smell, taste, touch and hearing.

But alas, all good things must come to an end.

From the founding of Rome in the 8th century BCE until the 4th or 5th centuries CE, Rome had been a multicultural society where religious co-existence and academic pursuits were the norm. Foreign religions were accepted and tolerated, as long as they didn't try to undermine the official state religion. It was the whole "when in Rome" thing.

However, this attitude changed in the 4th or 5th centuries CE as the first Christian emperors seized power. Theirs was a religion that demanded the worship of one male god only. All other gods, and the philosophies and rituals that attended their worship, had to go.

Even though most Romans still practiced the ancient faiths of their ancestors, these emperors enacted a brutal policy of Christianization that criminalized all other spiritual systems. In a world where the emperor's word was law, people of all classes had no choice but to fall into line.

Temples were vandalized and desecrated. Statues of the Vestal priestesses had their heads knocked off and crosses carved into their foreheads as the male-dominated Christian religion sought to strip women of power.

Those who honored the Flamma, even in the privacy of their own home, had their assets confiscated and were executed. The temple was ordered closed and the sacred fire was extinguished.

Despite widespread outcry and resistance, this policy of forced conversions and destruction of Classical culture finally achieved their goal – to wipe out the "old ways."

You might remember, however, that the Romans intuitively knew that their Eternal City depended on the Eternal Flame. Sadly, their intuition was right. Within a generation of the sacred fire being extinguished, the Roman Empire fell to invading armies.

Yet it wasn't just spiritual belief that was suppressed with the loss of Classical culture. As the world moved into the Dark Ages – that time dominated by the Catholic Church – humankind's "illuminated" pursuits were deemed heretical.

Science, medicine, philosophy, mathematics, astronomy, art and literature were acts of the devil. Only God had the answers. The ideas of secular law and women's rights were obliterated as the ideology of an androcentric, monotheistic institution wielded absolute power.

But what about the idea of human intuition? What about the intuitive perception and knowledge that humankind had embraced since pre-history and Firestarter's time? What about the spark of ancient intuition within each of us?

That too was extinguished as the church claimed that it, and only it, could reveal the truth of things unseen. It taught that humankind did not have the inherent capacity to understand itself and the universe. That kind of knowledge could only be given by God. And the church spoke for Him.

Accordingly, thousands of ancient scrolls – including those written by the likes of Plato, Aristotle and other scholars and poets – were burned and destroyed, literally turning centuries of human knowledge, history and intuition to ash.

But as we all know, the world keeps turning and what is taken by force cannot be held onto forever.

By the 14th century CE, the church's dominance had weakened as free-thinkers, humanists and enlightened Christians re-embraced the knowledge and intuitive teachings of the Classical Age.

Ancient scrolls – many of which had been hidden and preserved by forward-thinking priests and scholars – were rediscovered and their teachings again illuminated the world.

We call this period the Renaissance. It would mark the rebirth of critical thinking, discoveries in science and medicine, and the acceptance of intuitive knowledge.

It would also pave the way for the Enlightenment, that period where philosophers such as Immanuel Kant elaborated on the concept of intuition and intuitive awareness, thus building on the work of ancient Greek philosophers like Plato and Aristotle.

It's no accident that periods in human history are labelled the "Dark Ages" or the "Enlightenment." As a species, we have always associated darkness with ignorance and light with awareness. We still do. Darth Vader is the dark side of the Force. Luke Skywalker is the light side. You get it.

Perhaps we have Firestarter to thank for that. Perhaps we have Prometheus to thank, or Vesta's flame. Or perhaps we have the universe to thank as it banged its way into existence and waited patiently for us to evolve and see the light. Thank who you like, it matters not. The light is there.

When I met Camilla burning her aged beeswax candle at the ruins of a sacred hearth so many years ago, she was kind enough to talk to me about her ancient intuition and how the Flamma ignited it.

She also told me that this particular beeswax candle had been in her family for generations, and that she and her female ancestors had brought it to the ruins of the temple every year to relight it according to ancient custom.

In that way, the eternal flame of her faith – as well as the eternal flame of human intuition and awareness – had never truly gone out.

The embers of fire and the embers of intuition are very similar. Both have a remarkable ability to keep burning, even when they appear to have gone out.

As it happened, Camilla gave her candle to me. And as time went on in my life, its ancient flame would move me out of my own dark ages and into my own enlightenment.

You see, I've always been a skeptic. I've always needed evidence to believe in something. I grew up in a non-religious home and my reliance on evidence was only strengthened as I went through law school. If you can't prove it, it isn't real.

But a purely evidence-based life is a dark one. It acts like a self-imposed blindfold that stops us from seeing the bright colors and beauty that the universe so desperately wants to show us.

It stops us from seeing the magnificent sights that only our intuition can reveal. It stops us from seeing our true, whole selves standing in the light.

Intuition doesn't ask for evidence. It doesn't use rational thinking. It doesn't feel compelled to convince you of something beyond a reasonable doubt. If it were a lawyer, it would be a terrible one.

Yet I've come to learn that the voice of intuition is much wiser and often more useful than the voice of reason. Why is that?

Because reason depends on information that is known or knowable to us. That limits its depth, usefulness and accuracy, whether we're dealing with questions of science, metaphysics or a personal issue: *Should I do this or that? Why do I feel like this? What is the purpose of my life?*

After all, we don't always have sufficient information to understand a concept or make an informed decision in our life. We don't always have enough facts. That's when intuition is most valuable to us in a practical sense.

That's why the universe gave us ancient intuition in the first place. It fills in the gap between what we know or can know. It doesn't depend on anything. It *just knows.*

Your intuition *just knows,* too. It *just knows* in the same way that Firestarter *just knew* how to start a fire and *just knew* that enemies were lurking outside her cave in the night.

Your intuition *just knows* in the same way that Pythagoras *just knew* that a ^{2} + b ^{2} = c ^{2} and the Romans *just knew* their civilization would fall when the fire went out.

Even as you read this, you *just know* there is an untapped potential within you. And as you learn to ignite and control your ancient intuition, it will guide you to the awareness you seek and to the life you were meant to live.

PART II:

ANCIENT INTUITION,

AWARENESS

& ENERGY

Star-Stuff & Your Stuff

"Our Sun is a second- or third-generation star. All of the rocky and metallic material we stand on, the iron in our blood, the calcium in our teeth, the carbon in our genes were produced billions of years ago in the interior of a red giant star. **We are made of star-stuff.**"

- Carl Sagan

When Firestarter's daughter held up one of her mother's bones to the starry sky, implying that her soul had flown away – like a spark flies away from a fire – to become one with the stars, she was absolutely correct.

Of course, this *Home erectus* female wasn't educated in astronomy, cosmology, astrophysics, quantum physics or any other science. She had never read a science book. It would be another million years before the earliest refracting telescope would be invented by the species that evolved from hers.

Yet modern science confirms what she *just knew*. Our bodies are made of the same materials that the stars are made of. We are living, thinking, feeling human stars.

Carbon, nitrogen and oxygen, plus the atoms of other heavy elements such as calcium and iron, aren't just the puzzle pieces of stars, they're the puzzle pieces of our bodies, too.

It's no wonder that Carl Sagan, one of the most respected and knowledgeable scientists the world has known, stated in an episode of the television series *Cosmos* that:

"We are a way for the universe to know itself. Some part of our being knows this is where we came from. We long to return. And we can, because the cosmos is also within us."

Your body is a physical extension of the physical universe. Your body is part of the universe in a way that is both profoundly intimate and incomprehensibly expansive.

Firestarter's daughter knew that; however there was no way for her to know that – no way, that is, other than to *intuitively* know it.

Part of her being recognized the familiarity of the stars, recognized them as being an extension of her physical body. That recognition was planted into her – or rather into the material and energy that would eventually become her – at the birth of the universe itself.

At the moment Firestarter's daughter held her mother's bone up to the stars, her spark of cosmo-spiritual awareness may have seemed like a new one to her and her group. But it wasn't a new spark. It was in fact a very, very old one.

And that's what ancient intuition is all about.

Our pre-hominid ancestors and humans who lived in ancient times were far more familiar with the night sky than we are. Indigenous people created stories out of the stars, including the ancient Greeks and Romans who saw legends, people, monsters and magnificence in certain groups of stars, thus creating and naming the constellations.

When these people looked up, they sensed that what extended above was in some way an extension of their own life and experiences. They were curious about it. And you'll remember that curiosity is an integral part of intuition.

Curiosity is the tone our little voice takes when it wants us to explore something further. The exploration of the universe is thus an exploration of self. That's why I used a photograph from NASA and the Hubble Telescope in the artwork for this book's cover. When you look at a star, you're looking at a part of your self.

I want to share with you a popular Latin phrase used in ancient times: ad astra. It means "to the stars." The phrase is first seen in the Roman poet Virgil's poem *The Aeneid* and was written sic itur ad astra or "thus one journeys to the stars."

This is a popular phrase that you will still find used today in various capacities, often as a motto or mantra. A common expression is per asper ad astra. This means "through difficulty to the stars" or "it's a rough road to the stars."

I like this latter usage best because it can help put our struggles in perspective and can even bring meaning to very painful experiences. That's important, since the journey to become more intuitive can itself be a rough and uncertain one. It may be unchartered ground for you. Yet it's a journey that your ancient intuition compels you to undertake.

THE UNIVERSAL ENERGY
& YOUR ENERGY

You're heard the Shakespearean quote that, "A rose by any other name would smell as sweet." It articulates the idea that the words, names and labels we affix to certain items or ideas have no actual bearing on the true nature of those items or ideas. It also means that we can assign different words to identify the same or very similar item or idea.

For example, take the concept of universal energy. In ancient Sanskrit, the word used to identify the concept of universal energy or "life energy" is prana. The word refers to the cosmic energy that permeates the universe and our bodies.

Other words that mean essentially the same thing are chi in traditional Chinese culture, pneuma in ancient Greece, vitalism in Western esoteric circles and the Force in *Star Wars*.

This last bit isn't meant as a joke. It's the same idea – a life force that originates in the universe, one that permeates our being and binds us to each other and to the cosmos – and thanks to pop culture, it may be Yoda's explanation that is most easily understood by many people. That's okay.

The ancient intuitive knowledge that runs throughout these concepts is that life, on some level, is self-determining. The ancient intuitive knowledge these concepts all share is that the energy of life – the energy of *your* life – comes from the universe, exists within the universe, and survives what we perceive as the dying process to return to the universe.

Indeed, there is science to back this up. The most relevant is the first law of thermodynamics. Hang on – it's easier to grasp than it sounds. And it's important to know.

Basically, this is the law of the conservation of energy. It tells us that energy cannot be created or destroyed, but can only *change.*

That's why universal energy, which includes your life energy, is so tied into ancient intuition. For as our friend Aristotle said, "The energy of the mind is the essence of life."

Thus your ancient intuition and modern science are in complete agreement: Your energy and the universal energy are one and the same.

The heat energy that comes from fire is also part of this eternal energy. This is true whether it's a pre-historic fire, a fire in a temple's sacred hearth or the flickering flame of a simple beeswax candle sitting on your dresser.

Like you, fire is made of both matter and energy. It is a process more than a "thing." I think we would all agree that life is also a process more than a thing.

We are born, we grow, we live and we pass on. During the process...well, that's where things become unpredictable and uncertain. That's where you are right now. You're "in the process."

And just as the process of fire requires the wood or the beeswax to be consumed over time, so does the process of life require that your body be consumed over time. Yet neither the flame nor you can ever truly be extinguished. Both you and the flame are eternal.

So fear not. Your life energy – your thermal, mechanical, electrical, chemical, mental, emotional and spiritual energy – is in the universe's safekeeping.

I don't know about you, but I find that a beautifully comforting thought.

THE SCIENCE OF ANCIENT INTUITION: YES, IT'S REAL

Intuition may not care too much about science, but science certainly cares about it. Like intuition, science is curious in its own way: *So people can "just know" certain things? How does that work? How can that be useful to me?*

The phenomenon of the mind known as intuition is accepted in the scientific community. Not only do the best scientists believe in intuition, they actually rely upon it.

Albert Einstein famously stated:

"The intuitive mind is a sacred gift and the rational mind is a faithful servant."

What he meant by this is that intuition is the boss. It gets the big corner office in your brain and it gives the orders.

Rational thinking and actions are there to make intuition's vision come true. The scientific method (observation, hypothesis, prediction, experimentation and conclusion) is there to do the work that intuition dishes out.

Intuition is the spark that ignites the fire of rational thought and behavior. That makes sense. You must have a thought-idea-feeling before you can take the next steps: *Should I pursue this thought-idea-feeling? How can I give it substance or make it work? How can logic prove my intuition is correct?*

In this way, scientists are some of the most intuitive people around. They listen to their intuition when it tells them something about the world, and then they follow their intuition in a spirit of passionate yet rational discovery.

The famous economist John Maynard Keynes wrote that Isaac Newton's scientific revelations – which happened, of course, during the Renaissance – were due to his "intuition being the strongest and most enduring" that a human could be gifted with.

Most intelligent people recognize the central importance and catalyzing effects of intuition. You're here, right? You've sensed your intuitive self and you are now seeking steps to bring it into the light. Like any good scientist, you had a gut instinct and now you're exploring it further.

Speaking of that gut instinct – it isn't just an expression. Science has demonstrated that there are neurotransmitters in our "gut" that, like the neurotransmitters in our brain, respond to the stimuli of emotion (fear, love, joy) and environmental factors (a creepy parkade at night).

So when you say so-and-so makes your "stomach flip" or thinking about such-and-such gives you a "stomach ache," you're more right than you realize.

It isn't just you, me and the entire scientific community that recognizes the importance and usefulness of intuition. A few days ago, the police in my region advised the public to "trust their gut" (their words) when being pulled over, as there had been a report of a man impersonating a police officer and pulling over a female driver.

The constable applauded the woman, saying that her "spidey sense" alerted her to the fact that something wasn't right and she refused to get out of her vehicle. At that point, the man took off.

When I read this, I called my son over and made him read it, too. He is a superhero fan through and through, and I've often told him to listen to his "spidey sense."

In case you haven't heard the term, it's a reference to Spider-Man's ability to sense danger before it happens. I've often used this expression as a way to explain the idea of protective intuition to my son, and to urge him to trust his gut when something seems "not quite right" to him.

Yet intuition is ultimately a phenomenon of the mind, even if it engages our other bodily systems and senses. Science has shown us how the left side of the brain is ideal for things like law school, while the right side of the brain is ideal for art school. I'm generalizing, but you get the idea.

The left side of our brain is rational. It speaks the language of reason, evidence and judgment. The right side is more intuitive. It speaks the language of symbols, ideas and emotions.

A well-balanced person uses both sides in tandem, thereby engaging in whole-brain thinking. This is true, even though most of us gravitate toward one side or the other in terms of preference and ability.

We can also learn to use one side or the other depending on our needs. For example, you will want to engage left-side thinking when filing your taxes. You will want to engage your right-side thinking when deciding whether you still feel love for your partner.

On top of that, there's a fashionable idea that humans only use about ten percent of our brains, and that the vast majority of our mental and intuitive powers remain untapped.

This provocative idea may have come to us from an early 20th century book called *The Energies of Men*, written by a psychologist named William James. In it, he claims that people make use of only a small part of their potential.

Wow. Can you imagine what feats we'd accomplish if only we could tap into the other ninety percent? We'd all be superhuman.

Of course, brain scans have shown that our whole brain is engaged in even the simplest tasks like walking or eating. Yet that doesn't mean we're not using our brain to its full potential. In fact, I think very few of us ever do.

I'm suddenly reminded of an old *Far Side* cartoon. It shows a student sitting at his desk in a classroom. He has a tiny head on a large body, and his hand is raised as he asks permission to leave the room because his "brain is full."

It's funny, yes. But do our brains every really "fill up"? Of course not. As you've seen, we're made of the same stuff as the universe and the energy of the mind is limitless. We may be small, but we have big potential, particularly when it comes to our intuitive abilities.

Many women believe very strongly in "mother's intuition." I completely believe in this, and not just because I've heard about a gazillion women talk about it. I've experienced it many times.

For me, mother's intuition often presents as a dream. I distinctly remember an occasion when I dreamt that a necklace was wrapped very tightly around my throat. The sensation was vivid enough to wake me up, at which point I went to check on my son.

When I put my hand on his forehead, I discovered that he had a raging fever. He had been fine and symptom-free when he went to sleep, but a nasty case of strep throat had kicked in during the night. We ended up waking him up and taking him to the hospital that very moment.

But perhaps the most remarkable intuitive dream I've had happened during my pregnancy. I was about six months into my pregnancy when I had a dream that my son – I didn't know the gender at the time – looked like a tiny little doll about the size of a hamster. In the dream, he crawled up my arm (the same way a hamster does, if you've ever had one).

I plucked him off my arm and set him on a blanket, afraid to touch him because he was so frighteningly small. My mother appeared at my shoulder and said, "Don't be scared to touch your own child."

Well, as it happened, my son was born a month later, at the beginning of my seventh month. He was two full months premature and weighed only two pounds. For the next eight weeks, I lived with him in the hospital, learning to care for a preemie who was so small I could hold him in one hand.

And yes, there were many times I had to summon the courage to touch him. Not only was I terrified to hurt him by touching that tissue-thin red skin, but the tubes and lines and sensors on his tiny body were scary to navigate.

Many times I thought back to that dream and my mom's advice. "Don't be scared to touch your own child."

This latter dream is especially remarkable because it did more than just alert me to a current situation with my child. It actually predicted the future and gave me the intuitive knowledge of what was going to happen.

My intuition sensed what was going on not only with my body, but with the body inside my body. It was able to pick up on the earliest signals of distress in a way that my other senses could not possibly have done. At the time of the dream, I had no reason to fear the pregnancy was in trouble.

I credit this dream with keeping me on my toes during my pregnancy. As soon as I sensed something wasn't right with my pregnancy, I booked an OB/GYN consult at a renowned facility, even though it was in a different city and required travel.

Had I stayed in my smaller center, where OB/GYN was passable at best, I don't believe this story would have a happy ending.

While I absolutely credit the hospital's surgical, medical and nursing staff with saving my son's life – their skill and professionalism were second to none – I also think my mother's intuition had a big part to play.

Had I not experienced such a jolting and unforgettable dream, I might have brushed off that little voice telling me that something "wasn't quite right" with the baby.

I might have waited another few days to book an appointment, especially since I tend to put things off. Plus, I was doing my law articles at the time and was being pressured to attend to a full docket of clients.

Yet the doctors told me my son would not have survived another couple of days. I was admitted directly into the hospital during the appointment itself, on an urgent basis.

If you're a mother, you likely have your own stories of mother's intuition.

Perhaps you felt a sense of unease, only to receive a phone call from the school telling you that your son hurt himself on the playground or had been ill in class.

Perhaps you've been talking on the phone and felt an overwhelming desire to locate your daughter, only to find her talking to a stranger in a car on the front street.

Perhaps your child is an adult and out of the home, but you still pick up on those cues.

I know a woman who has learned to receive what she blithely calls "psychic twinkles" of intuitive knowledge. Recently, she had a psychic twinkle to visit her son, who is married with children.

Although it was out of character for her, she didn't tell him she was coming. She just got on a plane and went. When she arrived, she discovered that his wife was having an affair and her son really needed his mom's shoulder to cry on.

Interestingly enough, mother's intuition is reported across all cultures, and research has shown that mothers can predict the gender of their unborn babies.

We're fascinated by this, but we shouldn't be. We should accept it as naturally as we accept the verdict of the ultrasound saying "it's a boy" or "it's a girl."

For what could be more ancient and useful than mother's intuition? It is essential to the survival of the species. It is an unseen connection between mother and child, the most fundamental relationship in nature.

Yet we aren't just connected to our biological children. Our ancient intuition connects us to far more than those.

As the existence of mother's intuition continues to be empirically tested and proven in the medical and scientific fields, there is also a growing school of thought that says we are also connected – all of us, women and men – to our biological ancestors, living and dead.

To me, this is where things *really* start to get interesting. This theory posits that all humans carry slivers of our ancestors' experiences and knowledge in our own genetic makeup, and that those can be accessed by intuition.

Our genes don't just carry physical traits such as eye color or blood type. They do much more than that and the field of genetics is one of constant discovery. Yet most of us know that our genetic information – the blueprint of who we are – is encoded in our genes.

And yet "who we are" doesn't start with us. It starts generations back, with our distant ancestors. That's why the word "gene" is taken from the word "generation."

Have you always felt drawn to a certain place or time? It may be that your ancestor lived there or then. Have you ever wanted to do a family tree to discover your roots? It may be that a distant ancestor is calling out to be discovered. Perhaps he or she has something to tell you.

In a world where many people are estranged from immediate family, it can be very grounding and empowering for people to make this kind of connection with their more distant ancestors.

You come from somewhere. And I'm willing to bet the story of who you are is pretty damn cool.

I really think there's something to all of this. In the ancient world, Romans strictly adhered to a virtue called pietas. It referred to the divine devotion one had to his or her family, particularly as it related to "ancestor worship."

Romans kept the spirit and likeness of their dead ancestors alive by hanging casts called death masks (they were actually quite beautiful) of their ancestors around their family or personal shrine, called a lararium.

They also placed mementoes or tributes to these ancestors on their lararium, usually around a beeswax candle that burned with the sacred flame.

In times of trouble or moments of indecision, it was common practice for Roman men and women to kneel before this lararium and call upon the spirit of their ancestors for guidance.

As the candle's flame flickered, they would connect with those who had gone before and whose history and constitution was part of their own history and constitution.

This was ancient intuition in practice.

By accessing the energy of the flame's heat, by tapping into their own genetic makeup, these people were able to find the guidance they sought.

They became intuitively aware of centuries of knowledge accumulated by their own ancestors.

It follows that we can take all of this a step further. There is another school of thought – one I believe – that says humans have the ability to intuitively connect with all life, past and present. Not just human life, but all life.

All life, from the first organic simple cell that arose in the primordial soup of the early seas to the most complex evolved great ape reading this sentence.

Intuition is refined intelligence and instinct, and it comes to us from the universe through the evolutionary process.

It is encoded in our genetic makeup and it is passed on during evolution, adding more ancient intuition to our storehouse every step of the way.

Indeed, genetic research has proven that, despite the diversity of life on Earth, the genetic similarity of living organisms indicates the existence of a common ancestor for all known species.

Genealogical Tree of Humanity.

The Evolution of Man V.Ed.

PL.XX.

Man

Gorilla — Orang

Chimpanzee — Gibbon

Ungulates — Carnassia

Rodents — **Anthropoids** — Bats

Apes — Insectivora

Sirena — **Lemurs** — Cetacea

Marsupials

Promammals — Monotremes

Mammals

Teleostei — Theromorpha — Birds

Protopterus — **Reptiles** — Tortoises

Ceratodus — Crocodiles

Fishes — **Amphibia** — Lacertilia

Dipneusta — Serpents

Ganoida

Lamprey — **Selachii**

Hog — Cyclostomes — Amphioxus

Acrania

Vertebrates

Insects — Copelata — Ascidiae

Crustacea — **Prochordonia** — Thalidiae

Annelids — Tunicates

Echinoderms — **Articulates** — Rhyncocoela — Molluscs

Vermalia — Prosopygia

Cnidaria — **Platodes** — Strongylaria

Coelenterata — Rotatoria

Sponges

Gastraeads

Invertebrate Metazoa.

Rhizopoda — **Blastaeads** — Infusoria

Moraeads

Amoebae

Monera

Protozoa

E. Haeckel del.

That means all known species, extinct and alive. All known species, whether they lived in the past, present or whether they will live in the future as evolution continues.

The genealogical tree on the previous page illustrates this concept. We're at the top. But we didn't start there. We go back much further than Firestarter. We go back to cells.

Those cells lived. They didn't live like we do, but they are nonetheless part of our own history, both biologically and intuitively.

The trilobites lived, too. They didn't live like we do, but they are nonetheless part of our own history, both biologically and intuitively.

The same holds true of the first tetrapods (the four-legged darlings that first crawled out of the seas and breathed oxygen).

The same holds true of the promammals and the primates and the early hominids. They didn't live like we do – although they're getting closer – but they are nonetheless part of our own history, both biologically and intuitively.

How's *that* for a family tree?

Remember the truth of universal energy. The energy of ancient life is part of the energy of your modern life. As we've learned, energy cannot be created or destroyed, but only changed. That energy changed to become and interact with who you are.

That, combined with genetics and the evolutionary process, equips you with an intuitive awareness that reaches back some 4 billion years ago.

So now you can see that when I decided to call this book *Ancient Intuition*, I wasn't kidding around!

An Old Candle & A New Light
Believe the Buzz

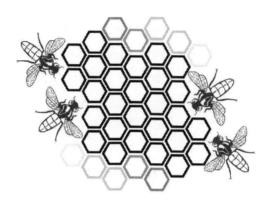

After Camilla gave me her old candle at the ruins of the ancient hearth in the spring of 1989, I thanked her and tucked it away in my backpack as I finished my travels through Italy.

When I returned home, it remained in my backpack for over twenty years, forgotten in my mom's basement among travel trinkets and regrettable 80's shoulder-padded shirts as I moved through university, marriage and motherhood.

It wasn't until the winter of 2012 that I was reminded of Camilla's candle and the things she had told me about the eternal flame.

This reminder came at a low time in my life, to be honest. I had been struggling with unhappiness and feelings of being unfulfilled. I didn't have a spiritual aspect to my life and that was starting to take its toll.

Again, this is a story I share in detail in *The New Vesta Secret*, but a quick telling will suffice here. During this time, my husband and I went to Las Vegas for my sister's wedding.

As we were wandering around, we stumbled upon a little wedding chapel with a mini temple that looked strikingly like the Temple of Vesta.

The sight brought it all back to me: the energy and freedom of my youth, the Via Sacra and the marble ruins of the temple, Camilla's voice, the sight of the candle burning near the ancient hearth, the power of the ancient flame.

It was that "coincidence" (more on these soon) that ignited in me the intuitive knowledge that this candle was something special. That it could illuminate something in me.

When we returned home from Vegas, I headed straight for my mom's house and excavated it from her basement. I hadn't seen or held it in over two decades.

For the first time, I noticed just how heavy this candle was and how the white "drapery" glass of the holder resembled the white folds of a Vestal's robes.

I noticed the age-darkened amber color of the wax and the imperfect way it sat in the container. I noticed tiny bits of debris – bee and hive bits – and I realized it was hand-poured: pure beeswax poured into an antique milk-glass bowl.

I had learned in university that the ancients used pure amber beeswax in candle-making because it was believed to be naturally pure in spirit and substance, just like the virgin goddess Vesta whom they believed resided in the flame.

And guess what? This ancient belief is completely correct. Science has now proven that burning pure beeswax candles in your home has a definite purifying effect on the air.

Unlike paraffin or soy candles, pure beeswax candles (those that are unbleached, dye and fragrance-free, and not cut with other waxes) create negative ions when they burn.

These negative ions do the same kind of thing that houseplants do: they neutralize harmful positive ions including dust and airborne toxins and common allergens. They purify the air to improve air quality and your heath.

So it seems that science can now prove what the ancients intuitively knew.

Yet I also remembered Camilla talking to me about intuition: "*L'intuizione delle donne*…when a woman has focus, she can see more. Flame gives that focus, you understand?"

At the time, I had nodded yes. That was a lie. At the time, I had no idea what she was talking about. Now I understand, though.

On March 1st, 2013 – twenty-four years to the day that I received the candle from Camilla – I re-lit it. March 1st is an auspicious day, you see. It is the traditional date on which the Vestals renewed the sacred flame in the temple.

Yet I knew the aged beeswax in the candle was generations old, so I wanted to find a way to both preserve it while at the same time spreading its flame.

Ultimately, I decided to light the candle only once a year, March 1st, according to ancient custom. I would let it burn for a short time and I would collect the melted beeswax so that I could add it to a new generation of beeswax candles that I would create and hand-pour in small batches each year.

Because I wanted my new candles to be as authentic as possible, I collected slabs of raw amber beeswax from a local apiary: as a pot of this new beeswax melted on my stove, I added a bit of the aged beeswax to it. (My eventual practice became to collect honeycomb cappings and render the beeswax myself. It's a long and messy process, but worth it.)

I then filled a number of round, clear glass containers with the mixture of the old and new beeswax. Round, to honor the circular shape of the temple. Clear glass, to allow the best view of the flame and beeswax as the candle burned.

For the crowning touch, I lit the wick of each new candle with the Flamma of the original candle. This was my way of carrying on the lineage of the Camilla's old candle and making sure that each new candle carried both the spirit and the substance of the original: the flame and the beeswax.

The only significant change I made was to create my candles with wooden wicks that crackled when they burned. The ancients believed the spirit of the fire – Vesta – spoke to them through the crackle of the burn. I still love this touch.

I began to burn this new generation of beeswax candles in my home. Eventually, more and more people began to ask me for one. Some of them wanted to embrace the ancient Vesta tradition as a home or personal spirituality.

But many others simply fell in love with the candle's amber glow, its soft heat energy, its vitalizing fragrance and its crackling wick. Each candle had a life of its own.

As I burned these beeswax candles in my home and life, I began to pick up on something. Or rather, I began to pick up on many somethings.

I began to become more intuitive. Not just a little more intuitive, but a lot more intuitive. I distinctly remember the first time it happened.

I was studying the wispy convolutions of the flame's vapor one afternoon when a thought formed in my mind. This thought formed in the same way that, if you look long enough at the clouds, you will eventually see a shape take form – an elegant swan, a tall ship, a bare-chested gladiator.

Okay, that last one is a bit salty, but you get the idea. The thought went something like this:

Don took his Volkswagen trike to work this morning. I hate that trike. I don't trust it. It's too old. It's just a matter of time until it breaks down and leaves him stranded, or worse. In fact, I can almost picture him on the side of the road right now...

But it's the middle of the afternoon, so that's impossible. He's at his desk, at work. Unless he's having an affair on me...then he wouldn't be at work. Man, I hate how paranoid I get when I have PMS. Still, something doesn't feel right. I'm going to call him.

I got up and dialed his work number. No answer. I dialed his cell number. This time, he answered – but his voice was heavy and labored. Like he was out of breath. Like he'd just rolled off his twenty-something cheerleader lover and was drained from sexual exertion.

"Where are you?" I asked.

"I'm...I'm..."

"Where?"

"I'm broken down on the side of the road," he said. "The engine in my trike blew."

"Why aren't you at work?"

"I was at work," he sighed heavily, "but there's a big storm moving in, so I wanted to get the trike home."

"Oh."

"I need you to hook up the trailer to the car and come get me."

It was a stressful drive to rescue him – I hate pulling a trailer behind the car – but it was also a trip full of revelation as I replayed Camilla's words in my mind.

"*L'intuizione delle donne*...when a woman has focus, she can see more."

It wasn't PMS paranoia that had put me on alert. It was real intuition. I was tapping into abilities I hadn't before used. So I made a conscious choice to start tapping into them.

I would focus on an important question – *Should I attend that conference in New York? Am I feeling healthy? Is my marriage strong?* – and then I would wait quietly and let my mind, spirit and body answer it.

I discovered how to "intuit" an answer to certain questions. As I knelt before the flame and placed my palms over it, as I felt its heat energy radiating into my being, I also felt my emotions and intelligence exploring the questions. I felt my gut instinct kick-in.

And the answer would form, just like a shape forms in the wisps of a cloud or the vapor of a flame.

Yes, I should go to New York…everything will be fine. No, I've been too sluggish; I need to start exercising more. Yes, my marriage is strong, but Don and I haven't had a getaway in months, and it's long overdue. Buy something sexy and book a room.

I could anticipate things better, too. It was as though I knew when Don was going to come home in a bad mood or our son was going to come home from school feeling melancholy. I knew it was going to happen before it happened, and I knew what to do about it. My intuition helped me connect to the people I loved in a deeper way.

In ancient times – long before we had smoke alarms, cell phones or social media alerts – I suspect that all of us were more naturally tuned-in to our intuition.

We had to be. We couldn't rely on a text message to alert us to danger, so we had to be open to receiving the message in a more organic way.

As my intuitive abilities grew stronger, I found that they weren't just focused on my family or specific questions or issues I was thinking about.

I soon discovered that spontaneous images, ideas and what I call "intuitive instructions" would pop into my mind during those times I was focused on the flame.

For example, I would be immersed in the sight, sound and heat energy of the flame, lost in inhaling the sweet fragrance of the beeswax, when suddenly I would feel compelled to get up – now! – and check my email.

So I'd get up and do it that moment, only to find an email alert that an online antiques auction was underway for a rare Roman coin I had been trying to find for years. With literally moments to spare, I was able to bid and win.

I would be kneeling or sitting before my Flamma candle, shutting out the rest of the world and my own thoughts, when suddenly I just knew the phone was going to ring or that someone was about to knock on my door.

That's the kind of thing that *never* happened to me before.

I also grew more perceptive of my own needs, whether they were to retreat for a quiet night or lose myself in a good belly-laugh. I knew how to stay happy and healthy. I knew what choices were in my best interests.

Soon, that type of self-intuition also expanded as I began to intuit more metaphysical matters.

What is my purpose? What happens when we die? What is the meaning of life? How does the universe work? I'm changing...what does it mean?

I might have assumed my newfound intuition was only coincidentally related to the burning of the beeswax candles, or that it was a "power of suggestion" thing; however, the feedback I got from others who were burning these candles convinced me that the cause and effect was definitely there.

First, this kind of feedback was completely unsolicited. I didn't ask for it and I didn't present leading questions about it.

Second, the feedback followed a very similar pattern. It started to come between two and three months after someone had received one of my beeswax candles.

People began to call or email me in excitement, telling me that they suspected this little candle packed a big punch in terms of sparking intuition.

They often began by talking about changes in their dream patterns. Many said they were dreaming more often and more vividly.

They could remember their dreams better and they found that their dreams were more understandable and relevant to what was going on in their lives.

They dreamed with purpose and found clarity and answers in the dreams. Some even had dream awareness, meaning that they were aware of when they were in the dream state and were able to manipulate it.

Soon after, the intuitive abilities began to appear in their waking lives, too. They *just knew* when the phone was going to ring or when a friend or family member was in trouble.

They arrived at decisions more easily, with less stress and regret and more certainty success. They picked up on things better.

And then soon after that, their intuitive selves began to ponder those more mystical, metaphysical questions that the human soul is so prone to ask.

They sensed their life was changing in some way. Some said they were "evolving." A few used the metaphor of a butterfly emerging from a cocoon.

But I knew it wasn't evolution. I knew the change came from looking back, way back, not moving forward. The change came from igniting the spark of ancient intuition that was already within them.

For me, and for many others, these beeswax candles provided the flame that ignited that spark of ancient intuition. I think their power comes in part from their lineage and the age of the beeswax taken from Camilla's candle. The reverence paid to that old candle, and the rituals performed around it for generations, were absorbed into the beeswax.

I also think these candles work because they link us to an age when fire – that symbol of eternity, the soul and the universal energy – was most revered by our species, and when its ritualized use was a part of daily life.

When we stopped lighting fires and candles and began flipping switches, we lost something. We lost the spark that keeps our ancient intuition alight.

Interestingly enough, science has something to say about all of this, too. Science has shown that burning beeswax candles stimulates the pituitary gland in humans which in turn triggers the intuitive parts of the brain.

Do you remember the night the thunderbolt struck the tree by Firestarter's cave? How it knocked the beehive from the branches and how the honeycomb melted in the flames, its amber beeswax spreading onto the ground?

The combination of fire and fragrant beeswax stimulated the intuitive part of her hominid brain.

In addition to stimulating intuition, the pituitary gland is involved in the conversion of food to energy. That means that burning a beeswax candle doesn't just make you more intuitive, it influences your own personal energy.

So as you can see, all of this helped me see an old candle in a new light. As importantly, it let me see my life and my ancient intuitive self in a new light.

You can see things in a new light, too. And this is the point where I'll ask you to strike the first match.

TO DO: As we move into Part III and especially Part IV of this book, we'll be focusing on practical application: that is, we'll be turning our attention to the steps you must take to both ignite the spark of your ancient intuition and to master it.

This will involve a number of intuition-igniting rituals that involve burning a beeswax candle. You will need one, so you may wish to start looking now in preparation.

I am still devoted to my annual March 1st candle-making ritual – I consider it a duty – and my wood wick, hand-poured beeswax Flamma lineage candles are occasionally available at FlammaVesta.com.

However, finding a normal pure beeswax candle and attributing meaning to it should similarly trigger your intuition. The science behind this is sound.

A heads-up here, though. The worldwide decline in honeybee populations means that pure beeswax candles can be expensive and hard to find. Do some shopping around.

You should especially be aware that there are no laws relating to accurate labelling of candles. The vast majority of candles labelled "pure beeswax" only contain a small amount of pure beeswax. Most manufacturers add soy wax or paraffin wax to bulk up the candle, and then add yellow dye to achieve a "natural" raw amber beeswax appearance.

They then slap a label on the candle that reads "pure beeswax" or "100% beeswax." Don't be fooled. Only 5% of such a candle may actually contain 100% beeswax! This is a shady practice, but it lets manufacturers make lots of inexpensive candles and advertise them as the real deal. Be sure of the product you're getting.

Your best bet may be to make a trip to a local apiary. That's what I do. I collect the cappings from the honeycomb and render the beeswax myself, just to make sure that I'm getting a pure product.

Yes, it's a time-consuming process, but it's essential to make sure you're getting the real thing. **Only a pure, uncut, unscented, undyed, unbleached and hand-filtered (no machines!) amber beeswax candle will spark intuition.**

Also, make certain that your beeswax candle has a **wood wick.** You will be using its distinct burn (the crackle, the embers on the wick, the unique heat energy etc.) during upcoming intuition-igniting rituals.

Finally, your beeswax candle should be housed in a **round, clear-glass container**. This will allow an unobstructed view of the amber beeswax as it burns and melts.

This round shape is a nod to the shape of the first ancient fires (Firestarter's circle of stones) and to the sacred hearth that burned in the Temple of Vesta.

ANCIENT AWARENESS
& THE AFTERLIFE

Seeing life in a new light is a good thing. But what about the afterlife? What happens when the energy of our life changes through the process we know as death? Isn't that the one question we're all dying to have answered?

It's been said that Edgar Allan Poe's poem *The Raven* is the most terrifying piece of literature ever written; however, it isn't the image of the ominous black bird perched above a chamber door that chills the blood. It's his message.

Open here I flung the shutter, when, with many a flirt and flutter,
In there stepped a stately raven of the saintly days of yore.
Not the least obeisance made he; not a minute stopped or stayed he;
But, with mien of lord or lady, perched above my chamber door -
Perched upon a bust of Pallas just above my chamber door -
Perched, and sat, and nothing more.

Then this ebony bird beguiling my sad fancy into smiling,
By the grave and stern decorum of the countenance it wore,
`Though thy crest be shorn and shaven, thou,' I said, `art sure no craven.
Ghastly grim and ancient raven wandering from the nightly shore -
Tell me what thy lordly name is on the Night's Plutonian shore!'
Quoth the raven, `Nevermore.'

Nevermore.

Once the black curtain of death descends, the Raven tells us, nevermore will we embrace those we love. Nevermore will we hear their voice or feel the warmth of their skin. Nevermore will we feel the warmth of a summer breeze on our face or feel laughter stir our soul.

It's a terrifying thought that fills us with a strange mixture of dread, panic, hopelessness and sorrow.

But remember what you've learned. Life, like fire, is a process driven by both matter and energy. The matter is the stuff of stars, while the energy is the universal energy that sustains us all.

A fire may go out, and yet its spirit goes on. The sparks fly off – we know not where – and the heat energy of the fire returns to the universal energy.

In the same way, a body may die, and yet its spirit goes on. The soul flies off – we know not where – and the energy of the body and mind return to the universe.

As I said previously, your life is in the universe's safekeeping. So are the lives of those you love. Your energies interact in this life and they interact in the afterlife, too. By afterlife, I simply mean what comes "after" the life we know.

Different people visualize or conceive of the "after" in different ways. Many people believe in reincarnation. Others believe in a type of heaven or nirvana. The ancient Romans believed in a place called the Elysian Fields, and this is my personal favorite conception of the afterlife.

It's a natural meadow where loved ones reunite in the afterlife to skip stones in the river during the day and sit by the fire at night. You can stay if you like. Or if you prefer, you can choose to live again in another form.

No matter how you conceive of the afterlife, remember that the universe knows what it's doing. It managed to create the stars and planets of countless galaxies, didn't it?

It managed to create an estimated 8.7 million species of life on our little blue-green planet alone, didn't it?

It managed to create about a gazillion known and still unknown natural systems of orbits, gravity, fusion, chemistry, biology, genetics and so on, didn't it?

Maybe we should cut it some slack and start trusting it.

Whenever Nevermore feelings kick in, I remind myself of a stanza from another poem. One that expresses what I know, deep down, to be true. One that my ancient intuition assures me is true: it comes from *Desiderata*, by Max Ehrmann:

You are a child of the universe, no less than the trees and the stars;
you have a right to be here.
And whether or not it is clear to you, no doubt the universe is unfolding as it should.

So as you make your way through eternity, even those parts of it that look like they end, take heart. Even if you've lost loved ones, take heart. Their energy is still around you. It surrounds you, different than their arms did and yet not so different. Even when the candle's flame goes out, does the heat not remain and flow into the space around you?

The memories of those you have lost or will lose, the love you felt or feel for each other, are forms of energy, too. The sight of a face, the sound of a voice, the sensation of a touch. They may seem transitory and insubstantial, but they are as eternal and sacred as the universe itself.

THE ANCIENT MESSAGE
OF "COINCIDENCE"

Just a few hours ago, before I sat down to write this section, I experienced what you might call a coincidence (isn't that a coincidence in itself?)

I was in the downstairs rec room chatting with my husband. He and our son had just returned from bringing an old bookshelf to the dump and he was setting up the new one.

We spoke for a few moments, and then I suddenly had the idea to sift through the stacks of old board games in the rec room closet.

There are the usual suspects there: Monopoly, Trouble, some playing cards and dominos, chess, backgammon, Operation, Battleship, Hungry Hippos (alas, missing all but two marbles) and Perfection. I went through all of these and a few more and then pulled out the Perfection box.

I took it upstairs where my son was sitting at the kitchen table, pulling off his mittens. I put the game on the table.

His jaw dropped. "Mom, I was *just* thinking about that exact game! I *just* saw a Perfection game in the garbage at the dump. I asked Dad if I could take it and he said no. He said it was dirty and you'd freak out."

Was this a meaningless coincidence? Was it just the intersection of completely random events and ideas?

Or was it something more?

I think it was something more. I think I was demonstrating intuitive awareness of what was on my son's mind.

I think the universe sent the energy of his experience, thoughts and emotions my way, and I intuitively picked up on them. It wasn't a coincidence, it was a connection.

In fact, I think many experiences that we see as coincidence are actually messages.

They are meant to tell us something or to draw our attention to something. They are meant to show us that there is a meaning, an order, to life.

They are meant to show us that there is a connection between our life and other things, whether those other things are people or not.

Yet it begs the question: What are the odds that, after probably five or six years of collecting dust, that Perfection game would simultaneously re-emerge in my life and in my son's life in such an unlikely and parallel way?

That isn't a question we need to answer. Coincidence isn't related to the odds or the laws of probability. It is related to intuition and energy.

All energy – which includes the energy of our thoughts, emotions and actions – is connected to the universal energy. Coincidence is a convergence of this energy for a purpose.

Coincidences have many purposes, but they almost always serve as messengers of some kind. Firestarter excelled at receiving these messages. It was no empty happenstance that a thunderbolt struck and ignited the tree next to her cave.

My Perfection coincidence was the universe telling me that I needed to slow down a little and spend more time "playing" with my kid.

I've experienced many other coincidences, too. Sometimes their purpose and meaning took a while to manifest in my life.

One such late-blooming coincidence became clear when I was teaching myself to create hand-poured candles back in 2012. I've never been a "crafty" person (the only class I ever failed was Home Economics!), so it was a bit of a gong show; however, I was determined to carry on the lineage of Camilla's Flamma Vesta candle by fusing the aged and the fresh beeswax in a new batch of candles.

I was working diligently at the stove, experimenting with the melting point of beeswax and the capillary action of wood wicks (and burning myself in the process), while Don was sitting at the kitchen table surfing the Internet.

"Did you know that there's an asteroid named Vesta?" he asked me. "It's called 4 Vesta. It has minor-planet designation and it's one of the largest asteroids in the solar system…in the asteroid belt between Jupiter and Mars."

I stopped pouring wax and looked at him. "No, I didn't know that."

"They named it Vesta because it's the brightest asteroid visible from Earth," he continued. He looked up from the computer. "It says here that Vesta was at its brightest magnitude in 1989."

"You're lying."

"Isn't that the year you met Camilla?"

"Yes, it is."

"Wow, what are the odds," he said.

Looking back at the big picture, I now know this was no coincidence.

Looking back, I now recognize that this was an alignment that heralded an important event, one that had great meaning, even though the meaning would take another couple of decades to become clear to me.

This asteroid "coincidence" was the universe sending me a message in its own cosmic language: *Pay attention, woman! This year is important in your life! I have a master plan for you!*

I'm sure you've experienced many coincidences in your life. Sometimes these messages are purposeful and focused.

You might be thinking about re-connecting with an old boss when, against all odds, you run into him in the middle of a hotel lobby in a city you're both visiting on business. And he offers you your dream job.

You might be wondering whether you should take a job in New York or Los Angeles, when you turn on the radio to hear Frank Sinatra belting out, "New York, New York!"

In fact, songs and music often feature into what people describe as a coincidence.

I remember many years ago, when I was in university and still single, my best friend and I were doing what single women do – talking about men – when she burst into tears and said, "I'm starting to believe that I'll never find love!"

At that very moment – literally that split second – Celine Dion's voice soared through the air of my tiny studio apartment, singing: "Love comes to those who believe it, and that's the way it is."

We laughed our faces off. The timing was perfect. It was like the singer was right there with us, sipping red wine and chiming in on our conversation in the most natural and fluid way possible.

Yet the coincidence changed our thinking. It really did. And perhaps it was no coincidence that I met my husband Don a month later. She met the man of her dreams the month after that.

Similarly, many people say that they are comforted by songs "coincidentally" playing on the radio or even in a store. I once remember going to lunch with a favorite colleague of mine whose mother had died a couple weeks earlier.

As we were eating and I was trying to cheer her up, she suddenly burst into tears.

A song was playing in the background at the restaurant (to this day, I cannot remember what it was) but it was her mother's favorite song and it brought back a flood of memories and emotions.

I felt awful for her; however, her response surprised me. She wiped her eyes with a napkin and said, "I haven't been able to cry since it happened," she said. "I really needed that." That was followed by a long, heavy sigh of relief.

Sometimes, however, coincidences are less purposeful or focused. Sometimes they're hard to understand or make sense of. Sometimes they leave us shaking our head, thinking, "What the hell was that all about?"

That's where our ancient intuition comes in. Remember that what seems to be a coincidence may in fact be a message. It may be a signal. You might have to do some fine tuning to hear it and make sense of it, though.

If you're of a certain vintage (as I am) you will remember the old-style radio dials, the ones you had to very carefully adjust by hand to pick up a radio station.

Turn it a wee bit to the left, static. Turn it a wee bit to the right, sound.

Coincidence can be like that. If at first you don't "get it," keep trying. Keep thinking. Keep turning that dial, intuitively moving it to the left or right.

The message might be faint, but if you keep scanning for it, it will eventually come through. Of course, it will come through on its own timeline. That might mean very quickly. That might mean weeks or months. Or it might mean years or decades.

But the signal, the message, will come through. When it does, be sure to crank up the volume. It might be the song you've been waiting your whole life to hear.

After all, coincidence is merely another intuitive tool in your inventory. It is merely one more way that your ancient intuition speaks to you, saying "Hey, you! Listen up. I have something to tell you. So pay attention to what's going on!"

THE UNIVERSAL LAW OF ATTRACTION

There is much talk today about the law of attraction. It has become a kind of pop culture phenomenon, a New Age get-rich-quick scheme: *Just concentrate on winning the lottery and you will! Just think hard about getting that new job and you will! Just focus on getting better and your tumor will disappear!*

Oh if it only it were that simple; however, the law of attraction isn't just wishful thinking. It isn't just "thinking positively." Positive thoughts are important and have great value in life, but the law of attraction is more than this.

The law of attraction is, like so many other things, a pattern created by the universal energy. It is a cause and effect pattern that our ancient intuition is well aware of.

Happily, we can learn to intuitively recognize the law of attraction on a conscious level, and put it to practical use in our lives.

In many ways, coincidence and the law of attraction are related. They are similar phenomena that work together.

As I said earlier, my Perfection coincidence was a message telling me to slow down a little and spend more time "playing" with my kid.

Yet here's the thing. I could have just said, "Wow what a coincidence," and then went off to finish up some client files or watch a re-run of the *X-Files*. I didn't have to find meaning in the message and I didn't have to act on it. But I did both. I acted in a way that "attracted" a better relationship between me and son.

The law of attraction is important because it gives us power. It gives us power to act on the message of coincidence, and to act on our intuitive awareness.

To a great extent – probably a much greater extent that we imagine – we can manipulate the energy in our lives via the law of attraction: the law of acting in certain ways and achieving certain results.

In my capacity as a couples' mediator, I often tell people that "like attracts like." Do you want to attract a quality partner? Start acting like a quality partner. Do you want your partner to appreciate you more? Show him or her more appreciation first. Those feelings will trigger a reciprocal action on his or her part.

I've experienced this kind of thing in my personal life. It was only when I accepted that "love comes to those who believe it" that I put out a completely different vibe in my love life. I believed it would come and it did.

Belief is an intuitive idea. It's a feeling. It's energy that you put out in one form, and that comes back to you in another form. This happens in all areas of your life. Friendships, family, work, finances, health and well-being, your interests and passions, spirituality, success and so on.

Think of it like this: the law of attraction is a sort of cosmic magnet. On one hand (or magnetic pole), it can attract certain things and circumstances to you, and on the other hand (or magnetic pole) it can repel them away from you.

A magnet attracts or repels by manipulating electrons and magnetic fields. In the same way, the law of attraction attracts or repels by manipulating your actions and the universal energy.

Do you want better grades in school? Attract better grades by putting out a magnetic pull that will draw them to you – study harder!

Do you want a healthier body and lifestyle? Attract good health by putting out a magnetic pull that will draw better health to you – eat better and get active!

Do you want to be happier in life? Attract happiness by putting out a magnetic pull that will draw happiness to you – spend more time with family and friends, indulge in your hobbies or passions, smile and learn to cope with stress!

Do you want to find more meaning in life? Attract meaning by putting out a magnetic pull that will draw meaning to you – help others, foster stray animals or consider quitting your job to "follow your calling."

Do you want to ignite the spark of ancient intuition that is already within you? Wait – you're doing that right now!

The law of attraction is great. Yet it is just one of many intuitive tools in your inventory.

It is one more way that your ancient intuition alerts you to a cosmic cause and effect pattern that you can manipulate to have the life you want.

MIND OVER MATTER:
HOW ANCIENT INTUITION
MANIFESTS IN YOUR MODERN LIFE

There's no doubt that picking up on the message of coincidence and utilizing the law of attraction by channeling your energies (putting out a magnetic pull that attracts desirable things to you) can change your life.

There's no doubt that these abilities are generated by a powerful source: your ancient intuition. And there's no doubt that the phenomenon of the mind known as intuition can manifest in your life in some very tangible, material ways.

Ancient intuition – or more accurately, the ability to ignite ancient intuition and see by its light – does give us the power of "mind over matter."

I strongly believe there is a link between our intuition and our physical state of being, both body and environment. I believe that we can manifest our reality more than we realize.

We've all done it to some extent. We've felt physical pain but, by controlling our thoughts and emotions, we've managed to control our pain impulses. That's classic mind over matter.

There are many times I've been teetering on the edge of a cold or flu as an important date loomed, whether it was a vacation or a media commitment. I know that I've talked myself out of getting sick, at least long enough to get through the event. *"You can't get sick now, Deb! You don't have time. Wait two days...then you can get sick."* I've managed to control my own immune system. That's classic mind over matter.

You've done it too, haven't you? You've willed something with all your mental, emotional, and intuitive might, and you've made it happen (or not happen).

But mind over matter also refers to prioritizing our intellectual and intuitive abilities over our physical abilities.

It's the whole "brains over brawn" thing. Do you put your money on the big, not-so-bright boxer or on the boxer who might not have as much bulk, but has ten times the brains? My money's on the latter guy.

Perhaps the best illustration of this is Firestarter. As an older female in a Stone Age hominid group, she was largely irrelevant and unimportant. She had no power and hadn't been "useful" to the group since her child-bearing years.

Nonetheless, her intuitive mind was superior to the matter of her body. Once she tapped into this, she changed her world and elevated her status. Humankind realized that the intuitive mind is the master while the body is the servant. Without that realization, there would be no human progress.

Do you remember the ancient Roman poet Virgil whom I mentioned earlier? He was the chap who coined the famous phrase sic itur ad astra or "thus one journeys to the stars" in his epic poem *The Aeneid*.

Well, he actually refers to this mind over matter concept in that same poem by saying, mens agitat molem which roughly translates to "the mind moves the mass."

Honestly, is there anything the ancients didn't know? It often seems like we're still catching up to them. That is especially true when it comes to igniting the spark of ancient intuition. Even Virgil – who lived and wrote in the 1st century BCE – owed his intuitive storytelling to the distant past.

"SHOULD I FOLLOW MY HEART OR TRUST MY GUT?"

At first glance, you might think that "following your heart" and "trusting your gut" are the same thing. They're both about listening to your intuition, right?

It depends. I think our heart – and by that I mean our desires and hopes – can definitely help us become more intuitive and make an intuitive decision or choice.

Yet here's the stumbling block with our heart. It can sometimes become too focused on what we *want* to do or what we *hope* (sometimes desperately hope) will happen.

As many of us have learned the hard way in life, if we desire or hope for something too strongly, those intense feelings can blur us to the reality of what's best for us.

That purely emotional or hopeful voice – *But I love him, I know it'll work out! I don't care about the rotting baseboards, I love this house! It doesn't matter what it costs, I need it* – can drown out the sound of our intuitive voice.

As a couples' mediator, I often see this play out in relationships. I will speak with someone who intuitively knows his or her partner will never change, or that the relationship is beyond repair, yet who still clings to false hope or an unhealthy type of "love."

Often, this person will rely on excuses to delay the inevitable decision he or she knows has to be made. *I can't leave her until she's finished the semester. I can't leave him until after his grandmother's birthday. I can't leave until I find someone to take my aquarium. I can't leave until I can afford a new couch.*

The excuses are sometimes so transparent they would be laughable if they weren't so sad and self-damaging.

Eventually, this person comes around. When he or she does, the expression is always along these lines: *"I knew in my gut it wouldn't work, but I kept hoping. I just loved him/her so much that I just didn't want to accept it was over."*

People do this in all areas of life. We know in our gut that we shouldn't buy that shiny black car with the suspicious knock under the hood – but wow, it's just so cute! That knock will go away on its own, right? Of course it will!

Yeah. Fast-forward a month and about a gazillion dollars in mechanics' fees and perhaps we're willing to admit the truth. *I knew in my gut it was the wrong decision.*

In fact, when I recently set out to buy a new car, my dad had some great advice for me: go car shopping when you're in a bad mood.

That seems counter-intuitive, doesn't it? But it isn't. In reality, that kind of approach often lets us hear our intuition clearly, without it being filtered by emotions that might mislead us or compel us to make an impulsive decision.

Yikes. Our gut can be a real buzz kill, can't it? Yes, but think of your gut as a genuine friend. As someone who will tell you what you *need* to hear, not just what you *want* to hear.

While both genders have the ability to trust their gut, I often find that men are particularly good at this. Even the expression "gut instinct" has a masculine ring to it, one that resonates with men.

It sometimes seems that intuition is closer to the surface for women than it is for men. Perhaps this is due to mother's intuition which, despite the advances we have made in technology and medicine, still plays a significant role in child-rearing. It's how we keep our children alive, especially when they're very little. Or perhaps this is due to women's intuition in general and society's acceptance of it.

Yet I've met and heard stories of many men who are profoundly intuitive and whose "gut instinct" serves them very well both in their personal and professional life.

Any successful businessman will tell you that his gut places a big part in his decision making. He doesn't buy, sell or trade based on the numbers alone. If the numbers look good but his gut tells him to hold off, he does. If the numbers are iffy but his gut tells him to take a risk, he does. And it pays off every time.

Think back to Firestarter's group. Do you remember when the young male from the neighboring group marveled at the number of kills the hunters had acquired? It was more than one group could even eat.

Once the spark of intuition had been ignited in Firestarter's group, its male hunters added gut instinct to their practical hunting skills.

They were able to sense and predict where an animal might be. There were able to conceptualize more complex hunting strategies instead of just relying on a luck-based "Hey, there's one – run and catch it!" approach.

Intuition in the form of gut instinct gives those men who have it a distinct advantage over those men who don't have it. That's as true in the modern digital age as it was in the Stone Age. It's as true on Wall Street as it was on the grassy fields beyond Firestarter's cave.

And men who learn how to access and master their gut instinct – that is, their ancient intuition – can channel that into whatever areas of life they choose, whether personal or professional.

To sum up, I'd say that in the best of circumstances, our heart and our gut tells us the same thing. We feel loving or hopeful or happy, and on top of that we have an intuitive gut sense of peace and confidence with our decision. Our stomach flips with true joy rather than churning with anxiety.

In the wake of a big personal or professional decision, we feel satisfied and content, rather than doubtful or stressed.

I've spoken to many people who assume "following your heart" is intuition. That's part of it, but your best bet is to achieve convergence where your heart and your gut are telling you the same thing.

WHY FAITH IS REALLY ANCIENT INTUITION

I remember sitting in an ancient religion class in university when a professor told us that there had been something like three thousand gods in recorded history.

I've thought about that often. To me, all of these religions are branches that stem from two common roots.

The first root is the human need for answers.

If you've spent any time around a child, you've seen this human behavior in action. *Why is the sky blue? What makes the wind blow? Why are there so many languages? Why did Fluffy have to die? Where is Fluffy now?*

Even as children, we want to be aware of how things work. We want to be aware of where we came from, of the meaning of our life and what happens to us after death. We want to be aware of the true nature of the universe and our place in it. We are intuitively curious creatures.

As adults, we want even more answers. We want even more awareness of things. We want a greater awareness of self and our own potential. We want to be aware of what decisions are best for us and how we can achieve a happy, fulfilling life, especially as the years go by faster and faster.

The second root is the human need for comfort.

It's the child that seeks a parent's embrace after the death of a pet, and who wants to be told that Fluffy is now out of pain and in a better place. It's the child that longs to hear the words, "Everything will be okay," from a parent, since that parent is the closest thing in their life to a god.

As adults, we still seek that kind of comfort; however, we stop seeing our parents as all-knowing omnipotent beings and we start looking elsewhere.

We want to be comforted that the universe is unfolding as it should. We want to be comforted that those fears of "nevermore" are false. We want to be comforted that we're making the right choices, that our life has meaning, that we can be happy and fulfilled, and that death isn't the end.

Wow. That's a pretty tall order, isn't it? To fill it, our species has come up with some pretty tall tales throughout our history. Don't get me wrong – there are many things about religion (past and present) that I find beautiful and I know it plays a big part in the lives of many people.

Yet I've long believed that religion and faith are actually alternate ways to access our ancient intuition.

By channeling our emotions, mental processes and physical actions into religious doctrine and ritual, we inadvertently feel, think and do the same things that are required to ignite the spark of our ancient intuition.

In so doing, we satisfy both of our primal needs: the need for awareness and the need for comfort.

When we experience the convergence of these two primal needs being met – when we feel both awareness and comfort – we experience a sense of reverence.

That is, we have a "religious experience." People who manage to hold onto that experience of convergence as they move through life often say that they "have faith."

Regardless of the religion they adhere to, such people can be quite intuitive. Deep prayer is not unlike meditation and it can have the same effect: to tap into intuition.

More fundamental religious practices, such as faith healings, produce a frantic state where some people undergo a mind over matter experience by feeling miraculously "cured."

The ideas and practices in *Ancient Intuition* can be used by those who hold a specific religious faith, whether Christian, pagan or anything else. You will find a way to reconcile them with your personal belief system.

However, this book may especially appeal to those who don't subscribe to supernatural-based religious belief and who wish to access their natural ancient intuition directly.

Even when I wrote *The New Vesta Secret: Finding the Flame of Faith, Home & Happiness* I wasn't sure that "faith" was the right word to use in the subtitle. It does the job and it is relevant, but it isn't exactly how I feel about it now.

Faith is belief. Awareness and comfort are achieved by believing a holy story. That works for many people.

Intuition, however, is knowledge. Awareness and comfort are achieved by intuitively knowing the nature of the universe and yourself.

It is the ancient holy knowledge that is already within you. It has its symbols – particularly fire – but in the end I think the words of yet another poet, this time William Wordsworth, say it best:

Faith is a passionate intuition.

PART III:

ACCESSING YOUR

ANCIENT INTUITION

ANXIETY, DIS-EASE, MISTAKES, UNHAPPINESS: HOW IGNORING YOUR INTUITION IS RUINING YOUR LIFE

You already know that being more intuitive will improve your life in many ways. We'll count the ways in a moment; however, let's spend a moment considering how ignoring your intuition can impact your life.

To that end, I'd like to share a story that I think illustrates this in a perfect yet unfortunate way.

Many years ago, I had a friendship with a great lady who on the outside appeared about as confident and independent as a woman can be.

On the inside, however, she was panicking as her "biological clock was ticking" and she was beginning to fear that she wouldn't have children.

To her friends, the panic was unjustified. She was in her mid-twenties and had plenty of time left. What was her hurry? Why rush the diaper years, we asked her. Live your life. It'll happen when it's supposed to happen. Don't rush it.

But she rushed it. She began dating a guy that everyone around her could see was a disaster waiting to happen. He scowled at her and stared at other women, often making her friends feel uncomfortable. He was creepy.

I knew her well enough to know that she didn't love him. It was a textbook case of "settling." In fact, if I remember right, it was she that ended up proposing to him. He couldn't be bothered.

A few weeks before her wedding, I did something that was completely out of character for me as I've always been a MYOB kind of person: I sent her a letter telling her that I was concerned about him, and that no one would blame her for slowing things down. (I didn't know until months later that she received two similar letters from other friends.)

But you know how this song ends. She married him. About a year later, the abuse started and, on top of it, some questionable sexual content was found on his work computer. The disaster hit.

During the storm of it, I remember her calling me on the phone. Through her tears, she told me something I never knew about the day she got married. She told me that as she was being driven to the church by a friend, she had a panic attack and began to cry.

Her friend pulled the car over and said, "You do not have to do this. I can make one phone call and the whole thing is called off. A few minutes of embarrassment will be better than years of regret. *Listen to your gut.*"

It sounds like a scene from a romantic comedy, doesn't it? Unfortunately, there was nothing funny about it. She didn't listen to her gut. She didn't listen to her intuitive voice which was saying, *screaming*, "Nooooo!"

Instead, she listened to other voices – urgency, panic, embarrassment, uncertainty – which were telling her that the caterer had already delivered the food to the reception hall. That her parents would be angry about the money they spent. That her family and friends would gossip about her. That she would never find another man, or at least wouldn't find one soon enough to have children. And so on and so forth.

Worse, these voices became so loud that she wouldn't leave him. Even after the police charges, even after the ugly revelations and disturbing behavior, she stayed with him.

I wasn't the only one to end our friendship because of it. It's hard to see someone spiral like that. Any connection you had to them disappears.

Instead of enjoying or re-embracing her life as a healthy and happy single woman, she ended up wasting decades of her life with a shell of a man who treated her like something stuck to the bottom of his shoe. That kind of relationship eats the soul from within.

But that's what happens when we don't listen to our intuition. That's what happens when we silence it, stomp on it, shut the door on it.

A feeling of dis-ease, whether experienced as an acute panic attack or as chronic low-level anxiety, is perhaps the most common way our intuition waves a red flag at us.

We've all felt it. Most of us have ignored it at some point as well, and always to our down detriment.

Many years ago my husband took a job transfer to a northern city. It was a good move in terms of his career, as it was a promotion; however, we hated the town. It was isolated and its oil and gas foundation meant it had a fairly transient population of young workers coming and going.

My husband was content renting a nice condo until we saw how things would pan out; however, I started pushing him to buy a house.

Everyone told me not to. Even my parents – who are normally phenomenal at minding their own business – told me not to. "Don't tie yourself to the place," they said. "The real estate market is too unpredictable. You'll lose money."

Did I listen? Of course not.

I didn't listen to my intuition either, although it was doing everything short of taking out a billboard on every street corner to get my attention.

I felt a palpable sense of dis-ease. My heart was pounding, my head felt heavy and even my breathing was off. Still, I went ahead with it.

I went ahead, even though I hated the town and knew I'd want to move. I went ahead, even though I knew the real estate market was wonky and we'd lose money. I went ahead, even though I knew Don didn't want to buy a house there and was only desperately trying to make me happy.

It was short-sighted, impulsive and counter-intuitive in the extreme. And I cannot tell you how loud my intuitive voice was speaking to me at the time. Shouting at me.

Stomach aches. Tears. Trembling limbs. Even as I signed the papers, my heart was in my throat. And as soon as the sale went through, I remember sitting on the steps of my new house and crying into my hands.

"I feel like we made a mistake," I said to Don.

But it wasn't our mistake. It was my mistake. And I'll bet you know how this song ends, too.

We lived there for only ten months before the bottom fell out of the energy sector and we moved, selling the house at a shocking loss. It took a toll on our bank account but it also took a toll on our marriage. Don is too gracious a man to admit it, but I know he had lingering resentment about it.

This begs the question: *Why do we sometimes work so damn hard to ignore our intuition, even when it is deafening and we know we should listen to it?*

Now that's the million dollar question.

I've asked myself that question, and I've answered it.

Looking back, I desperately missed the house we sold in our previous city. I wanted the same sense of security and pride that comes from home ownership. I thought – hoped – that owning instead of renting would make me feel more at home and happy with where we were living.

Once I started the process of house-shopping, I think I kind of got caught up in the momentum of it, like being swept away in a current that I had created and yet couldn't stop.

That was partly due to youth and inexperience. I hadn't lived long enough to have a made a big financial mistake yet, so I didn't have that experience to draw on. (You can bet I have it now, though!)

I also think I was "settling" for a life in the same way that my friend was settling for a husband. I was trying to force something. To make happiness, security and fulfillment happen by sheer force of will.

Of course, it doesn't happen like that. I know now that I can only achieve happiness, security and fulfillment by listening to my intuitive self.

You won't achieve happiness, security and fulfillment until you listen to your intuitive self. But you already know that, don't you? That's why you're here. That's why you're starting to ignite the spark of ancient intuition within you.

Here's the weird thing, though. I've come to realize that that feeling of dis-ease, whether experienced as an acute panic attack or as chronic low-level anxiety, isn't a bad thing.

It's a good thing. Why? Because it gives us a clear message. *Don't do it!* Because it gives us an opportunity to slow down, to re-think, to re-group and to re-order our lives in the way that *will* make us feel secure, happy and fulfilled.

"How Will Being More Intuitive Change My Life?"

Many people live in a chronic state of uncertainty. I see this in my work all the time. It's the spouse who says, "I don't know if my wife has left her lover," or "I don't know if my husband still loves me."

This uncertainty exists in many areas of life. It's the woman who wonders, "Will I beat this illness?" or "Will I have enough money to enjoy my retirement?" or "How can I find joy?" It's the man who wonders, "Should I take that job?" or "Should I get on that plane?"

It's all of us wondering, "What's the purpose of my life? My life is changing...what does it mean? What should I do? How can I understand the plan the universe has for me? How can I know my true self and find the happiness I seek?"

At times, we are keenly aware of this uncertainty. That is especially true during times of crisis or transition.

Yet many of us have become so accustomed to living in a perpetual state of underlying uncertainty that we have come to accept it as a "normal" way of existing.

We simply don't know any different. The curtains are closed and we don't even know they can be opened to reveal the blue sky outside.

But take heart.

Your ancient intuitive awareness, the awareness planted within you by the universe, is the antidote to the uncertainty you are suffering in your life today.

It delivers this antidote in three ways.

First, it alerts us to the uncertainty itself by giving us those feelings of dis-ease, whether we experience them as a sudden panic attack or a chronic low-level of anxiety in our lives, or as something else.

Second, it guides us to the right answers in a practical, real-world and problem-solving way. (You will learn how to master this process in this part and in Part IV.)

That is, it advises us how to best fight an illness, how to save money, how to find joy, how to discover our true self, and so on. It's kind of like having your own personal guru/banker/physician/counselor/psychic all in one.

The third way your ancient intuition delivers the antidote to uncertainty is more ethereal: it provides you with an intuitive awareness of the universe itself.

Once you are able to find meaning in life, once you are able to know your true self and the plan the universe has for you, you can find peace. You can find answers and comfort.

You become certain of things. Your mind, body and spirit are wrapped in a blanket of certainty that "the universe is unfolding as it should."

Certainty – whether about life, relationships, money, the soul or true self, the cosmos, the future – can only be illuminated by the spark of ancient intuition within you.

That spark will change your life in every way. It will change – for the better – your relationships, your finances, your emotional and physical health, and your future.

It will transform a life full of uncertainties to one full of certainties. You will be certain of what actions are in your best interests. You will be certain of your true self and your place in the universe. You will be certain that you will achieve your true potential and get the most out of life.

LOOK FOR MEANING – IT'S LOOKING FOR YOU!

It's human nature to look for meaning in life. We like to say, "Everything happens for a reason." I believe that; however, it can sometimes be tricky to discover that reason.

Unfortunately, however, we too often (and too desperately) look for meaning in people, places or things. We think marrying a certain person or buying a certain house will give us that meaning. It rarely does.

I've worked with very wealthy, high-profile people who seemed to "have it all." The perfect spouse, the perfect home, the perfect body, the perfect career. Yet these people were some of the unhappiest, most *uncertain* people I've met. Some of them struggled long and hard to find meaning in life.

That's because true meaning can only be intuitively acquired. It cannot be physically, matrimonially or financially acquired. Trying to find meaning in a particular person or a particular object is like treating an illness with the wrong medicine. In some cases, it simply doesn't have any effect. In other cases, it makes matters much worse and causes a host of other ills.

Trying to acquire inner awareness from an outside source is like trying to find a fish in the desert sands. You're simply not looking in the right place.

Jump into the ocean, however, and the waters suddenly teem with what you're looking for.

One of the first steps toward igniting the spark of ancient intuition within you is to look for meaning – rather, to search for and scrutinize meaning – in your day to day life.

That is, to search for and scrutinize the meaningful connections or coincidences in your life. Looking for meaning in what appears to be meaningless. Look for substance in what appears to be insubstantial.

Be the metaphysical-minded mathematician of your own life, discovering meaningful patterns within what appears to be the abstract chaos of life's twists and turns.

Look for the design behind the coincidence, and the correlation between seemingly unrelated events or facts.

For example, my birthday is January 31st. Big deal, right? Well, there is actually some meaning there. January is named after the Roman god Janus: the god of new beginnings, since January is the first month in the new year.

Janus is depicted as having two faces: one looking forward toward the future, the other looking back, toward the past.

I have been told that January 31st is an auspicious and meaningful day because it is the last day of the first month. It has been divined that a person born on this day will spend their life both "looking ahead while looking to the past."

And that perfectly sums up my life.

As an avid Classicist, I am always looking to the ancient past; however, I am also dedicated to bringing ancient knowledge to the modern and future world. That's the whole purpose of the book you're reading!

Where the month and day of my birth were formerly meaningless – just a random intersection of time when my mom's uterus kicked in and kicked me out – they now have profound meaning. I can see the purpose of my life reflected in them.

The same thing goes for my name: Debra. It means the "bee." What a weird and random meaning for a name, right? Yet now it makes perfect sense and has profound meaning in my life. I spend a lot of time working with beeswax. Doing so is a fundamental part of my life.

In fact, this bee-related endeavor is what first ignited the spark of ancient intuition within myself.

Could my parents have predicted this when they named me? Of course not. But the universe could and did.

An easy and accessible way to find meaning in your life is to get curious about the events and facts that occur and exist within your day to day life.

Think back to Firestarter and her group. The discovery of fire sparked a certain *meaningful* curiosity in all of them and they began to find new meaning in life.

If they could learn to control life, didn't that mean they could learn to control other things, like the trees or the animals...or the entire world?

Remember – burn it into your memory! – that curiosity is an integral part of your ancient intuition. The universe wants you to get curious about it!

The universe wants you to know its secrets on an intuitive level. It wants to re-establish its ancient connection with you – you, a spark of its eternal fire and a wandering fragment of its universal energy. It wants to tell you about the life plan it has for you.

Yet while you're looking for this pre-destined and ancient meaning in your life, remember also to actively create new meaning in your life.

The universe may have planted its own seeds within you, but it left you plenty of fertile ground to plant your own.

ANCIENT INTUITION:
BODY, MIND & SOUL

We intuitively know that mind is greater than matter: think back to Virgil's phrase, mens agitat molem (the mind moves the mass.) We also intuitively know that the soul can fly out of the body to rejoin the universal energy, like a spark flying out of a fire.

Yet this kind of hierarchy where the body is essentially subordinated to the mind and especially the soul cannot be too rigidly adhered to when we are trying to tap into our ancient intuition.

For the purposes of becoming more intuitive in both an active and a passive sense (more on this soon), we need to take a holistic approach to body, mind and soul. That is, we need to have all three working together toward the common goal of igniting the spark of our ancient intuition.

Just as the temple housed the eternal fire, so does your body house your eternal soul. Just as wood fueled the sacred energy that burned within, so does thought, emotion and sustenance fuel the sacred energy that burns within you.

We've already looked at the ways ignoring or being unable to tap into your intuition can affect the physical body in very real ways. Dis-ease, anxiety, stomach aches, stress headaches and even more serious illness can result when we aren't tuned-in to our intuitive self.

When we are tuned-in to our intuitive self, however, we take better care of our body, which in turn allows it to take better care of our mind and soul.

So take care of yourself! Treat your body like the temple it is. Nourish it with good food. Treat it well by exercising regularly and caring for your skin, hair and teeth. Get regular medical check-ups.

Treat your body tenderly by getting enough sleep. This is especially important since a good sleep state is essential for intuitive dreams to form. See the connection? Your mindful, intuitive self can only develop in a well-rested body.

To this end, many people find that listening to "white noise" during the night facilitates a good sleep state while simultaneously setting the ideal conditions for intuitive dreaming.

It does this by creating a sort of sound cocoon which insulates the dreaming body and mind from distracting noises, whether it's a dripping faucet, the honk of a car outside, a pet's nocturnal movements or whatever. It creates a very soothing aura that is highly conducive to sleep.

White noise sound machines are relatively inexpensive and are widely available online, as well as in wellness stores and department stores.

Part of caring for your body includes learning to understand "body language." I'm not talking about the way your cross your legs or roll your eyes, here.

Rather, I'm talking about the way your body speaks to you. It speaks to you through physical sensations. It alerts you to something bad through anxiety, stomach aches, chest tightness, pain and so on.

At the same time, it alerts you to something good through what we often call the "warm fuzzies." That's the warmth of serotonin, the so-called happiness hormone secreted when you feel joy or contentment.

Take care of your mental and emotional state, too. Relax and enjoy more milk baths. Don't jump for the phone during dinner – let it go to voicemail. Learn to care less (a lot less) about what people think of you.

Nurture friendships that soften your heart, and distance yourself from ones that harden your heart. Spend time doing what you love, whether it's bird-watching or reading or playing video games. Learn something new to keep that brain of yours challenged and curious about life.

At the same time, learn to understand the language that your mind and emotions use to send you a message. That's an essential part of becoming intuitive.

We've already looked at the ways ignoring or being unable to tap into your intuition can affect your mental and emotional well-being in some very real ways.

Making mistakes in life (i.e. marrying the wrong person, making impulse purchases, etc.) is an unfortunate consequence of ignoring our intuitive self. These can cause us great mental distress and emotional trauma.

To tap into your ancient intuition, you *must* identify and remove those factors that are causing mental or emotional discord in your life. They are barriers to your intuitive self.

Yet don't be surprised if those factors that are causing you mental and/or emotional discord are also causing you physical discord.

The example that comes to my mind is that of a female client whose formerly close friendships were deteriorating.

She said that her two closest friends had withdrawn from her quite a bit in the last few months. The interactions they did have had become chilly and distant. This was causing her great mental distress and emotional pain.

On top of it, she had gained a lot of weight and was feeling very down on herself about that. Her physical energy and sense of well-being were very low. Her mental and emotional energy and sense of well-being (about both her life and friendships) were even lower.

As it turns out, it was all connected. She had begun to "let herself go" physically, which really took its toll on her emotional and mental states. To put it plainly, she hated how she looked and she began to hate herself for it.

Soon, she began to bow out of her friend's invitations. Every time they asked her to go bike riding or meet for lunch, she said no. She wasn't feeling good in her own skin.

It didn't take long for her friends to take the rejection personally. They began to withdraw from her and stopped inviting her to join them for their usual outings.

Eventually, my client and I were able to cut through the hurt and assumptions, and she realized the first domino that fell in this situation was her failure to follow her intuition.

She ignored her little voice when it told her to start taking better care of herself, especially physically.

She ignored her little voice when it said, "Hey you! Don't you see how tired you are all the time? Don't you see how everyone but you is out having a good time? You know you have to do something. So do something!"

I think this situation illustrates how the mind-body-soul distinction is somewhat arbitrary and artificial. Our thoughts, emotions, physical well-being and our spirit are all deeply interconnected.

They're pieces of the same puzzle, even if we conceive of them as looking very different. In order to see the big picture, we need all three to fit together seamlessly.

That's why I encourage you to take a holistic approach as you begin to tap into your intuitive self. You need your mind, body and soul working together toward the common goal of igniting the spark of ancient intuition within you. Take care of all aspects of your being.

Before we move on, I'd like you to do some serious introspection. Let me ask you: What factors in your life are causing you physical, mental or emotional distress?

Think about that question for a while. Write down the answers on a piece of paper, if you like. This is an important first step in the intuitive process.

You must realize that feelings of physical, mental or emotional distress are messengers. They exist to alert you to a situation that has to change for your own good.

Your body, mind and soul want to be balanced. When that balance is off, you're going to wobble. You're going to feel "not quite right" in any number of ways, whether a stress headache, a period of depression or anxiety, insomnia, or even compromised mental functioning where you find yourself always forgetting things or unable to think clearly.

You may also see the effects seep into other areas of your life, such as your interpersonal relationships or your work. You may even blame other people or circumstances for an imbalance that is actually originating within yourself.

Strive for clarity and to get to the root of your imbalance. Don't automatically assume that a partner, friendship, job or situation is to blame for your imbalance.

Before you place that kind of blame, crank up the volume of your little voice and listen hard. Has it been trying to tell you something about your own body, mind or spirit? Does the work have to begin with you? It may or may not. I'm simply suggesting that you ask that question before you start pointing fingers at other people or circumstances.

At the same time, it is possible that an outside source is the root cause of your emotional, mental or physical distress.

If you truly feel that an outside source – a person, place or situation – is causing the imbalance, you will need to take real measures to separate or insulate yourself from them.

But here's the thing – if your intuitive skills aren't yet strong enough, you may not be able to determine what factors in your life are causing you physical, mental or emotional distress. You might try to figure it out, but come up empty.

That's okay. Don't panic. Your ancient intuitive self knows the answers. Even better, it got the answers from the ultimate authority: the universe. And it desperately wants to pass on those answers to you.

Soon, we'll be focusing on real-world practices and principles that will ignite the spark of ancient intuition within you. These are daily/nightly activities and attitudes that will illuminate the answers to every question you've ever asked.

Passive vs. Active Intuition

You know those "send" and "answer" buttons on your smartphone? You know what they do, right? Of course you do. One lets you make a call, one lets you receive a call.

Intuition has send and answer buttons, too.

Many of us have received a call from our little voice. It might speak to us through an intuitive feeling or thought, or through an intuitive physiological response such as a sense of anxiety or contentment. It might speak to us through a coincidence or a seemingly spontaneous idea.

That's passive intuition. Your intuitive self is reaching out to you. Whether or not you answer it or listen to its advice is another matter. Either way, you're on the receiving end.

Active intuition is something else. It's where you reach out – or rather into – your intuition. It's where you actively call upon your intuitive self for some reason, most commonly to seek an answer to a question you have in life.

Of the two, passive intuition is arguably easier to master; however, that doesn't mean it doesn't take practice to perfect it or that it is less valuable to you in life. It just means that, by its very nature of being the initiator, it is simpler to recognize and utilize.

To oversimplify, passive intuition requires you to open yourself up and receive. It requires you to be on alert for intuitive messages (i.e. coincidences, gut feelings and mental, emotional or physical dis-ease) and to receive and process them. It takes some work to receive these intuitive messages loudly and clearly, and to accept them as truth.

Active intuition, on the other hand, requires you to initiate the intuitive process on a conscious and subconscious level. It requires you to actively utilize your thoughts, emotions and physiological sensations to "scan" for certain information or answers that dwell within your ancient intuitive self. It takes more work and skillful focus to master this ability.

When it comes to passive versus active intuition, one isn't better than the other. They are both invaluable to you. Depending on the circumstance, you may choose to use either one, or both, of them in unison.

As you strive to master passive and especially active intuition – a process you will begin to do in few more pages – remember to have patience. Don't force it. Get rid of any sense of urgency. There's no rush. It will happen!

As you move through the lessons in the upcoming "How to be More Intuitive in One Month: 30 Daily Practices & Principles" section, and as you commit to working through and mastering the five-step process in Part IV (Five Steps to Ignite the Spark of Ancient Awareness Already Within You), your intuition will develop in an organic way.

It will develop naturally, like the way you naturally awaken from sleep to the sound of chirping birds. It won't happen suddenly. It won't jolt you awake like the obnoxious buzzer of an alarm clock. So work hard. Be patient.

After all, just stop and think about what you're learning to do! You're learning to extract information from the most ancient part of your life. You're learning to extract information from the most ancient part of the universe itself.

And when I say *ancient*, I really mean it.

Astronomers tell us that the universe is around 14 billion years old (they can determine this by looking for the oldest stars and measuring the rate of the expansion, extrapolating back to the Big Bang).

For some 14 billion years, the universe has been expanding. Now it's your turn to expand. It's your turn to expand your intuitive awareness of your place within that ancient and ever expanding universe.

For some 14 billion years, the universe has been delighting in its own energy. Now it's your turn to delight in your own energy. It's your turn to claim your portion of the ancient universal energy and to use it as you wish.

The universe might be very old, but it's also very patient. It's been waiting for you, another of its beloved children, another sacred spark from its eternal fire, to come home. To be curious. To understand. To do the work it takes.

So take a breath. Relax. Begin this journey toward your ancient intuitive self with patience, perspective and passion. It isn't a passing fad. It is your new way of existing. It is your new lifestyle on a daily and nightly basis.

Commit – this very moment – to immersing yourself in the upcoming daily practices and principles that will help illuminate your intuitive self. Commit – this very moment – to diligently working through the five-step process in Part IV that will ignite your ancient intuitive nature.

Borrow a little spark of dedication and patience from the infinitely patient universe, if you must. Why not? You've already borrowed the material of your flesh and bone, and the energy of your thoughts, emotions, soul and intuitive self.

The universe isn't just patient. It's pretty generous, too.

THE FLAMMA & INTUITIVE FUSION

The word "fusion" has a common meaning as well as a scientific meaning. Here's what the dictionary has to say:

Definition of FUSION (Merriam-Webster)

2 : a union by or as if by melting: as
   a: a merging of diverse, distinct or separate elements into a unified whole
3 : the union of atomic nuclei to form heavier nuclei resulting in the release of enormous quantities of energy when certain light elements unite

When most of us talk about fusion, we are talking about an idea and a process: the idea and the process of combining different substances or concepts – from food ingredients to political ideologies and everything in between – to create something new and distinct.

As we go through life, we learn to fuse our interests, feelings, knowledge and beliefs with other interests, feelings, knowledge and beliefs. Life is a process that thrives on fusion.

One of my best friends is a devout Catholic; however, she has still managed to fuse her very orthodox religious beliefs with the natural spirituality of her intuitive self.

If you think about it, there are probably many ways you've used this kind of fusion to create the life you have, and to create the person that you are.

When you use fusion in this way, you are using energy. You are combining the energy of your life's various aspects to create the unique person you are and the unique life you have.

As you go through the process of life – as you grow and age – you have naturally learned to fuse your knowledge, experiences, emotions, ideas, thoughts, beliefs, behaviors – together.

Part of this happened subconsciously. That's called growing up. It was, at least in part, a passive experience.

But part of it happened consciously. I'm sure there have been many times you have had to actively engage all of your mental and emotive powers to move forward in life.

But what about your intuition? Have you actively engaged it? Has the energy of your ancient intuitive self "fused" with the ancient energy of the universe?

Well, that's precisely what's going to happen here. Fusion is the means by which you will ignite the spark of ancient intuition within you. Fusion is the means by which that wayward spark that is you will rejoin the eternal fire.

You see, the universe is a big fan of fusion. It loves it. The universe loves it so much that it uses the process of fusion to power the billions upon billions upon billions of stars that illuminate its darkest corners. Fusion powers our sun – all suns – and is the energy that makes all life possible.

This energy is produced by fusing two light atoms (hydrogen and deuterium) together at the crazy high pressures and hot temperatures at the sun's core – something like a toasty 15 million degrees Celsius – to create a new atom (helium).

As it happens, the amount of energy needed to hold this new larger atom together is less than the total energy that was needed to hold the two original atoms together. The excess energy is released in an electromagnetic wave.

Clear as mud? Good. My goal isn't to teach you the intricacies of nuclear fusion in our sun. Rather, my goal is to illustrate that the process of fusion is as important to the infinite ancient universe as it is to the person sitting and reading this book.

You both use its principles in your own ways. You both use its energy, too. Actually, you share its energy.

And just as the universe uses the process of fusion to illuminate and sustain its ancient starry self, so too will you use the process of fusion to illuminate and sustain your ancient intuitive self.

To do this, you will need a focused source of energy.

A while back, I gave you the task of finding a pure, uncut, undyed, non-fragranced amber beeswax candle. Ideally, it should be housed in a round clear-glass container and have a wood wick. (Again: if you cannot find an authentic beeswax candle, visit an apiary to create your own from honeycomb cappings or visit FlammaVesta.com.)

It is this candle that will provide the focused source of energy that you will use to illuminate and sustain your ancient intuitive self.

You'll also be using this candle to work through many of the daily intuition-sparking practices and principles in the next section, as well as the five-step process in Part IV.

There are several reasons we'll be using a beeswax candle in this way. First and foremost, it works. It has worked for me and for many, many others.

You will also remember that pure, uncut and non-fragranced amber beeswax has been scientifically proven to stimulate the pituitary gland, which in turn enhances the intuitive centers of the brain. We know this works and its effects cannot be underestimated.

In addition, we know that the ancients used beeswax to burn candles in their homes. This substance has a long history of illuminating lives and spirits in both a practical and a metaphysical sense.

Importantly, fire is symbolic of eternity, the universe, the soul and the intuitive self. It is a light in the darkness. It is a process, like fusion, and like our own lives.

As we go through life, we change and adapt just as fire changes and adapts to the shifting wood. As we move through death, we change yet again. The soul flies out of the body like a spark flies out of the fire, both off to rejoin the universal energy.

As you followed Firestarter's story at the beginning of this book, you saw how the sight, sound and heat energy of fire stirred the first feelings of reverence in the human spirit.

You saw through Firestarter's eyes how fire worship became humanity's first religion and how it made us intuitively aware of our own sacredness within the sacred universe.

You saw through her eyes how the flickering flame made our species intuitively aware that we are *more*. That there is *more* to the story of life than the cover at each end.

You saw how it sparked our curiosity. Our desire to look for meaning. To pull order out of the chaos. To explore the universe within us and the universe beyond us. To become *more*.

And then you came along as we traveled through time from the Stone Age to proto-history, and to Prometheus's gift of fire and intuitive awareness.

As time went on, you saw how Firestarter's rough but sacred circle of ancient stones evolved into the sacred circle of marble that was the Temple of Vesta, and how the flames that burned within each, although separated by millennia, were from the same eternal fire.

You have felt that eternal fire warm your own spirit. You've felt it no different than Firestarter, or the Vestal priestesses or the billions of humans who have lived and died upon this Earth. There's nothing like the heat from a fire. Nothing else has the power to simultaneously soothe and illuminate the soul.

Nothing else reminds us – through its flickering flames, crackling and roaring sound, and radiating heat energy – that we are more than matter. When we are illuminated and warmed by fire, we intuitively know this about ourselves. There is a little bit of Firestarter in each and every one of us.

If you've ever stood by a fire or sat close to a candle's flame, you know what I'm talking about. You've felt the heat energy of fire radiate into your body, to fuse with the energy of your being.

Go ahead, try it now. Get your candle and light it. I'm serious…get up and do it.

Now hold your hands over the flame, just low enough to feel its heat energy radiate into your palms. Feel how its heat energy enters you to fuse with your energy.

It is that heat energy that you will consciously fuse with – particularly during the five-step process in Part IV – to ignite your intuitive self. This process is called "intuitive fusion." And the Flamma of your beeswax candle will provide the energy and focus to make it happen in your life.

How To Be More Intuitive In One Month:

30 Daily Practices & Principles

The purpose of this important section is to do some groundwork that will prepare you for the five-step process in Part IV and make your intuitive journey a successful one.

Just as a student must know the subject before taking a test, just as a runner must be well-conditioned before running the race, so too must you be familiar with the daily practices and principles that will help ignite the spark of ancient intuition already within you.

While this section presents quite a bit of new information, it also quickly revisits a few previous concepts. I wanted to present you here with a comprehensive inventory of the everyday thoughts, behaviors and philosophies that will prepare your mind, body and spirit to fuse with your ancient intuitive self.

Earlier, I encouraged you to be patient during the process of learning to engage your intuition, both passively and actively. I asked you to commit to making it your new way of living in a long-term and holistic way.

To that end, I would like you to spend one month preparing for the five-step process in Part IV. During that month, you will regularly review the content presented so far in this book by flipping back through its pages.

You will also work your way through the 30 daily practices and principles presented in this section. You don't have to do these in any particular order; however, be sure to check off or make a note of them as you move through them, so that you don't miss any.

I also recommend that you regularly re-read those daily practices and principles you've checked off so that all of this content stays fresh in your mind. Remember, we are taking a holistic and long-term approach to this. Learn to access your ancient intuition in a comprehensive and consistent way.

Too many of us live fragmented lives. We might be doing okay in one part of our life, say work or relationships, but then suffering in another, say physical health or spiritual well-being.

We might feel sound in mind, body and spirit but feel we are still "missing something." That is often the intuitive aspect of our being. To become whole, to become more intuitive and at one with ourselves and the universe, we need to first mend and heal those fragmented parts of ourselves.

In the most practical terms, this often translates to breaking bad habits and forming good habits. This isn't oversimplifying matters. It is absolutely essential. The ancient philosopher Aristotle said:

> "We are what we repeatedly do.
> Excellence, therefore, is not an act, but a habit."

Isn't that the truth. Having good or bad habits can make or break us, regardless of what we're trying to do.

How we habitually relate to our family or friends, what we habitually eat for meals, whether we habitually exercise, if we habitually choose to have a positive or negative outlook in life…all of these things form our personality, yes, but they also determine our strengths and weaknesses and our overall quality of life.

People who relate well to others – who are easygoing, mindful of others' feelings but still respectful of their own boundaries – tend to have healthy relationships.

People who eat well and exercise tend to enjoy a healthier, more active life. People who focus on the positive (as much as possible) rather than the negative tend to be happier and less stressed in life.

When we choose to habitually engage in the thoughts and behaviors that are most likely to attract the lifestyle we want, we are essentially practicing the law of attraction.

We can also use our habitual thoughts and behaviors – as well as the law of attraction – to ignite, develop and master our ancient intuition.

But before we can forge new good habits, we might have to break some old bad habits.

Think: what habits are holding you back from opening up your mind, body and spirit to your intuitive self? That is, what habits stand in the way of clarity and contentment?

It could be anything. It could be habitually calling a friend whom we know only has negative things to say and who has a way of knocking the wind out of our sails. It could be wasting hours watching TV or surfing our time away online, caught up in the false world of social media.

It could be diving into the cookie jar when we're emotional, thereby using food to either soothe our sorrow or stress, or share in our joy. It could be a habit of falling into emotional outbursts or turmoil, whether anger, accusation, tears, indignation or self-loathing.

Once you identify your bad habit(s), the next step is to ask yourself this question: Why do I want to break this habit?

That's a good question, isn't it? Often, we readily see our bad habits and immediately start trying to break them in a variety of ways. In so doing, we miss the essential step of knowing *why* we want to break those bad habits.

We miss the essential step of imagining what our life will look like a year from now if we *don't* break the habit versus how it will look if we *do* break the habit.

We rush the process by jumping to problem-solving – *I'll put carrots in the fridge instead of cheesecake! I'll stop talking to so-and-so! I'll learn to control my anger!* – without taking the time to let our intuitive self get a good look at the bigger picture.

By jumping to problem-solving, we don't think through the issue enough to have clarity or to muster the motivation we will need to make changes last in the long-term.

It's hard to break bad habits. To do it, and to make those changes stick, you must know why you are doing it. You must have a clear vision of how your life will be happier and more meaningful when you're free of those bad habits.

Once you have taken those initial steps of a) identifying your bad habits and b) knowing why you want to break them and forecasting how your life will look when you do, you can move on to the next step by c) problem-solving by figuring out how to actually break the habit in a practical way.

Sometimes, we are motivated enough by that image of our bad-habit-free lifestyle that it's reasonably easy to break the bad habit. We just need to remind ourselves daily of our goal, and perhaps reinforce that by having some visual reminders to keep us on track.

Some people leave sticky notes around the house to mentally and emotionally stay "in the zone" of breaking a bad habit. These may express messages of encouragement.

Other people write a word on their hand or wear an elastic band around their wrist so that they can "snap" themselves out of it – both figuratively and literally! – when they feel tempted to fall back into destructive habits.

These kinds of constant visual reminders can help keep our motivation strong and our momentum going, so that we consistently avoid falling back into the rut of negative thought patterns, emotions or behaviors.

In my work as a couples' mediator, I work with many people who are trying to break bad habits. One of the more common bad habits is speaking with a negative voice tone. Not only does this make us come across unpleasantly to our family and friends, it has a tremendously nasty impact on our own emotions.

When encouraging a client to break this particular bad habit, I often recommend a somewhat bizarre strategy to my female clients. I suggest that they wear a color of nail polish that they wouldn't normally choose.

Sounds silly, right? Perhaps. But it works like a charm. Think about it: just about every move you make during your day requires you to use your hands. You are constantly seeing them, right in front of your eyes and peripherally.

Seeing this constant flash of jarring color in your line of sight can help you stay "in the zone" of breaking negative behaviors, thought patterns or emotional responses.

As a woman is helping her kids with their homework, she remembers to remain patient and use an encouraging voice tone each time she points to something in their textbook.

As a woman goes through her work day and speaks to her colleagues, as she drives home and speaks to a friend on her car phone, she sees her hands moving before her and remembers to keep her attitude and voice tone positive.

As a result, she leaves everyone with a better impression of her. She feels better, too. Much better. Her improved voice tone has improved her mood.

For many women, it's kind of fun to approach change in this colorful way. Breaking a habit and forging a new lifestyle for yourself should be fun!

Another way to remain motivated and keep your momentum going is to change your external environment to reflect the changes you want to make in your internal environment – that is, to your behavior, thoughts or feelings.

Have you been thinking about painting your walls a different color? Now's the time.

Have you been thinking about redecorating your living room or updating your kitchen or bedroom? Now's the time.

These changes don't have to be big or expensive, either. Burn inexpensive incense. Shop for a different tablecloth or a few unique decorations at your local thrift store.

Carry the changes over into your daily activities. Choose a different type of tea or coffee. Change your hair or personal style. Make a change that says – *I'm making a change!*

In the spirit of that positive change, let's move on to focus on those various daily practices and principles that will ignite the spark of ancient intuition with you. I've presented them (again, in no particular order), as follows below.

As I said earlier, these cover a wide and diverse range of ideas, attitudes and actions that will help prepare you to be more intuitive in thirty days.

If you wish, you can read through them all at once to get a good overview of what's coming up. You may find that you want to put these practices and principles in an order that works for you, and that can help strengthen any areas of your life that you recognize as being weak.

After that, however, you should focus on one practice or principle every day, for one month.

The more you can master these practices and principles, the easier it will be to master the five-step process in Part IV and ignite the spark of your ancient intuition.

A CHECKLIST OF DAILY PRACTICES & PRINCIPLES

• **A morning mantra**. Have an affirming and meaningful word or phrase that you say and/or read to yourself each morning shortly after you awake. This word or phrase should remind you of the changes you want to make and of your commitment to illuminating your intuitive self.

This word or phrase – a mini pep talk – will help you establish your all-day focus by starting the day off in a positive and very conscious way.

- **Active observation**. Get curious! Look around yourself as you go through your day. As the saying goes, "Stop and smell the roses." But I mean it literally. Stop. Smell the roses.

Notice how the blue the sky is. Notice how green the grass is and how red or orange the flowers are. Notice how your child's eyes sparkle when he or she laughs. Notice how your friend lights up when you compliment her or him.

Notice how a warm breeze or a chilly wind feels against your face. Notice the black canopy of night and how the stars shine like diamonds in the sky.

Notice the iridescent green of a dragonfly's eye or the metallic blue of its body, and notice how you can hear the flutter of its wings as it flies by you.

Notice the interactions and conversations of those around you as you stand in line for your coffee. Notice what books people are reading.

Notice what music is playing. Everything that happens around you is energy and you can learn to read that energy by actively observing it.

Time flies. Notice that, too. Notice how your thoughts, emotions, behaviors and your physical body have changed and continue to change as you age.

Embrace it. It's okay to get older – or rather to appear as though you're getting older. All of us, including you, are no older and no younger than the universe itself. Age is energy, and your energy is eternal.

Notice life's fine print, its tiniest details, and get curious about those. Remember that curiosity is an integral part of igniting your intuitive abilities.

The universe wants you to notice it. It wants you to observe and understand it. Curiosity is its invitation. So accept it!

• **Challenge coincidences**. Remember that your ancient intuition is the code-breaker the universe has given you to discover its secrets.

Intuition gives us the power and insight to pull order out of disorder and to organize what appears to be disorganized.

It shows us that what appears to be abstract or disjointed is in fact meaningful and intact.

Be on alert for coincides and, when they happen, scrutinize them. Challenge the notion that they are random or meaningless, and instead accept that they are by design and full of meaning. Look for that meaning. You'll find it.

• **Manifest the life you want**. Remember that your mind has power over the matter of, and in, your life.

Focus your thoughts and emotions on the reality you want to create, whether it's a state of mind (i.e. more peace, greater happiness, enhanced self-awareness, etc.) or a state of being (i.e. a better relationship, more financial security, a healthier body, etc.).

Recognizing the power of mind over matter is a core aspect of creating your intuitive self.

• **Practice holistic healing and health.** Don't compartmentalize your life by regarding the mind, body and soul as distinct. Think holistically by taking care of yourself mentally, emotionally, physical and spiritually. You will need your "whole self" to ignite your intuitive self.

In the same way, don't compartmentalize your life into work, home, family, friends, hobbies, values, and so on. Strive to have a holistic attitude so that you can "be yourself" and enhance your intuitive self regardless of where you are, what you're doing, or who you're doing it with.

• **Take micro-breaks.** It's all too easy for the day's distractions, worries, stresses and demands to overwhelm us and knock us off-track. Don't let this happen.

Every hour, be sure to stop what you're doing and take a two-minute micro-break. Take a few deep, grounding breaths to relax your body. Visualize something or someone that makes you happy.

If you sit for most of the day, stand up and have a good, long stretch or run up and down a flight of stairs. Just move. If you move for the most of the day, sit down and have a few moments of restful peace.

If your environment is conducive, light a candle and spend a minute or two in relaxing reflection as you let the flame soothe your spirit.

If you can't light a candle, a good substitute is an LED flameless tea light that you can turn on at your work station. Choose one that has an amber (instead of a white) "flame."

- **Recognize the connection between your thoughts, emotions and actions.** Most of us recognize that our thoughts can influence the way we feel. When we think about something happy, we feel happy. And vice versa.

But our actions can also influence the way we feel and think. We can behave our way to a better mood. In fact, "acting" happy can sometimes make us feel happier and have happier thoughts.

"Acting" in a loving way can sometimes make us feel more loving and have more loving thoughts.

This is important thing to know because it is sometimes easier to change or control our behavior than it is to change or control our thinking or emoting.

Here's an example: the summer before I wrote this book, my family and I went to Kananaskis – a park system in the Rocky Mountains – to go trail-riding on our bikes. One afternoon, Don stayed in the hotel to have a nap while my son and I went off bike-riding through the mountain trails.

I spotted a few signs around the area that warned, "Grizzly bear spotted in the area. STAY OFF such-and-such trail," but I didn't pay them much attention. I didn't think we were near such-and-such trail (my map-reading skills suck). Plus, signs like that are nothing new in that part of the world.

Letting my son take the lead, I chased him up and down various trails until we arrived at a river. We dropped our bikes and spent some time throwing rocks into it.

Tiring of the river, my son focused his rock-throwing efforts on hitting a nearby trail sign. That's what thirteen year old boys do. It was only when he hit the sign that both of us actually read it and realized where we were.

That's right: we were on such-and-such trail.

"Mom," he said, "we're goners." His face was already white and he was staring into the thick forest all around us.

I felt a thud of panic. He looked at me.

But then a stroke of genius hit me. "What, are you chicken?" I said, *forcing* my voice to take on an adventurous tone. "I have the bear spray. There's nothing to be worried about. But let's race back and tell dad…we'll be able to tell everyone we were almost eaten by a grizzly bear."

He loved it. We hopped onto our bikes and took off. Stark terror was transformed into an adventurous spirit.

That transformation happened through my behavior alone. By the way I handled it, by the actions I took and the voice tone I used, I almost convinced myself that it was fun!

I almost convinced myself that a canister of bear spray the size of a Bic lighter would be sufficient to ward off a 1500 pound Grizzly bear that stood nine feet high on its hind legs.

By the time we got back to the resort, we were giddy with laughter. Of course, I engaged in some serious self-loathing afterward, but my point is this: our behavior, the way we physically respond to a situation, can influence our mental thoughts and emotions.

We can convince ourselves to be calm, happy, optimistic, whatever, by the way we behave.

If you're finding it a struggle to have more positive feelings or thoughts, try to let your actions take the lead by behaving in more positive ways.

Force yourself to do it, if you must. Force yourself to smile, to watch something funny, to go for a walk or exercise, to call a good friend and reconnect. Do this every day.

This approach is consistent with taking a holistic approach to the mind, body and spirit. When one is weak, the others can compensate and provide the strength you need to get you where you want to go.

A final word here, though. To do this, you will need to keep your motivation in mind. My motivation in that moment was to keep my son from feeling afraid, and to keep control of the situation. What's your motivation? Clearly it is to access and master your intuitive self. But why do you want to do that? Answer that question, and you'll have the motivation you need.

• **Have a boss phrase.** Do you know what a "boss fight" is? It's a climactic fight in a video game where your character must battle and destroy a particularly big and powerful opponent to move forward in the game (or to "level up"). It usually takes a few tries to do it, but once you manage it, you have the satisfaction of having overcome significant obstacles so that you can be the boss, so to speak.

I want you to have your own boss phrase. This is kind of like your morning mantra; however, it is a very short phrase that you can repeat to yourself whenever you feel you're slipping into bad habits, thoughts, emotions or behaviors during your day.

The goal of repeating this boss phrase is to remind yourself that have overcome obstacles in your life and that you will continue to overcome them. You have the power. You have the strength. You're the boss. And if you want to "level up" to your intuitive self, you have to remember that.

• **Exercise.** Have you ever heard of a "runner's high"? Basically, it's a state of euphoria experienced not just by runners, but by anyone engaged in a vigorous activity.

It is thought that this feeling of euphoria is caused by the release of endorphins (sometimes called the opiates of the brain) during periods of intense physical activity.

It is common for celebrity inspirational speakers and life gurus, including those who teach "transformational" life strategies, to use this natural occurrence for their purposes.

For example, I remember a colleague of mine attending a "transformational event" where the speaker claimed to have the power to "electrify" each participant's sales potential.

Following this claim, he had everyone in attendance stand up and dance for approximately fifteen minutes as a loud, bouncy, inspirational song played in the auditorium.

By the time the dance-fest was over and the participants took their seats, their brain and blood were saturated with activity-induced endorphins. They felt euphoric and new sales ideas were flourishing in their minds.

And the speaker took all the credit, claiming his patented technique had opened the door to such feelings of well-being, creativity and clarity, and that in the process he had transformed their sales potential.

But the speaker didn't do it. Each individual participant did it. You can do it, too. Exercise isn't just good for the body, it's good for the mind and soul. It provides feelings that simultaneously comfort, inspire and pleasure.

Add physical activity to your daily routine. Do it to provide your body, mind and spirit with a flood of feel-good endorphins. Your intuition will thrive in such a space.

- **Create a lararium.** The ancient Romans who practiced fire worship in the form of honoring their goddess Vesta had a type of personal shrine, called a lararium, located near the entrance to their home.

Even if they don't know where this custom comes from, many people already have something similar in their home. It's that long table with framed family photos and mementos.

If you don't have such an item, consider adding one of these to your home: it can serve as a visual reminder to remain committed to igniting the spark of intuition within you.

It can also be a very lovely and comforting thing to have in your home, and can have whatever spiritual meaning you attribute to it.

A lararium can be modest, even as simple as a shelf, cabinet or table top. It can also be more elaborate and take the shape of a traditional or rounded Greco-Roman temple, like the Temple of Vesta that housed the sacred flame.

It may or may not have doors. A lararium with one or two front doors, hinged to open and close, can preserve the privacy of this personal place of spiritual focus.

This personal shrine can be classical or modern, home-made or manufactured. Some people prefer their lararium to stand out from the rest of the home's décor, while others prefer that it blend into the home's furnishings and fashion.

A beeswax candle that symbolizes the Flamma should be placed in the center of the lararium.

Around it, you can place items that remind you of the people or things you love. Many people will set items from a lost one's life (from wrenches to dog collars) on their lararium to keep that person's or animal's energy in the home.

Many people also place items that they believe enhance their intuition on their lararium.

Because the Temple of Vesta was traditionally adorned with laurels, a fun option is to grow an indoor herb garden, one that contains a bay herb, on your lararium. Plant it in a Roman-style pot to complete the theme.

Potted flowers or flowering cactus gardens are also nice additions and can add colorful "life" to this space.

Regardless of how you decorate it, be sure to create a lararium that you love and that reflects your style, flair and personality.

It should make you happy whenever you look at it, and should remind you of the things that are most important to you.

It should be the last thing you see when you leave the house, and the first thing you see when you get back home.

Other than the one constant – the presence of a Flamma candle in the center – use your own fashion sense and have some fun with it.

Whether it is created on a wooden cabinet, glass table or even a wine cart, the lararium is your personal sacred space. Do what looks and feels right to you.

• **Nourish the flame.** I mentioned earlier that the ancients who honored the sacred Flamma would customarily sprinkle offerings of salted flour or libations of olive oil or milk into the fire of their household hearth or into a candle's flame. This was a symbolic way to "nourish" the flame while also nourishing their own mind, body, spirit and intuitive self.

You can practice this beautiful ancient custom in a similar way. During meal-times, as well as during times of prayer or silent meditation, place a shallow bowl of loose salted-flour, olive oil or milk beside a burning Flamma candle.

(Some people still sprinkle offerings or libations into a candle's flame; however, leaving them in a bowl by the candle provides a cleaner and safer burn. If you choose to sprinkle into the flame, always remove debris from the cooled wax.)

Another option is to create offerings in the form of intact wafers by blending flour, salt and water together, shaping into round wafers, and baking briefly in the oven.

You can then pass a wafer over the candle's flame during meal-time, or during times of prayer or silent meditation, to symbolically nourish the flame and your self.

(Note: you will need at least one of these salted-flour wafers during the five-step process in Part IV.)

This lovely ancient ritual can help you stay focused on your goal of illuminating your intuitive self while providing daily ritualized comfort and inspiration.

An interesting side note: these sacramental wafers were baked by the Vestals in antiquity and offered to their fiery goddess. After closing the Temple of Vesta, the Catholic church claimed these as their own Communion wafers.

• **Be honest**. Be honest with yourself. Deception of any kind – and especially self-deception – clouds the mind and heart, stresses the body, and stifles the intuitive process.

Becoming more intuitive isn't just about adopting new behaviors, it's also about abandoning old self-destructive behaviors. You intuitive self needs a healthy space to grow in.

• **Tune out to tune in**. We live in an increasingly angry, sanctimonious and cynical society. Negativity is everywhere and sometimes it seems that everyone is out to make us as miserable as they are.

Accessing your ancient intuitive self requires clarity and contentment (among other things). To achieve these, you will have to learn how to "tune out" the belligerent world so that you can "tune in" to your beautiful self.

The more you listen to other people's voices, the less you will be able to hear the "little voice" of your intuition.

Get a bit of a chip on your shoulder! Know that you're following the path that is right for you, and learn to ignore the haters out there. Realize that their negativity or cruelty has more to do with their life than yours. It is a reflection of who they are, not who you are.

• **Be content with who you are today.** We live in a superficial, consumer society where we're never quite "good enough." We're never young enough, rich enough, attractive enough, thin enough, interesting enough and so on.

Bullshit. You are enough.

Stop putting your life on hold or waiting for tomorrow, hoping things will be better when you're thinner, richer, married, divorced, have kids, have the kids leave home, buy a house, sell a house, etc.

Your ancient intuitive self has a message for you:

You are good enough. You are a child of the universe. Don't change. Just get to know your whole, true self as you are now.

• **Have a spa day every day.** No, I don't mean this literally. Most people don't have the time or resources to book a spa appointment every single day.

Yet most of us have a daily shower or bath: and with a little prep work, you can transform this daily or nightly activity into a relaxing and reinvigorating experience for the mind, body and soul.

Illuminate your bathroom with candlelight. Play some spa music in the background. Indulge in fragrant body washes or bath salts, as well as luxurious towels.

Slow down. Instead of jumping in and out of the shower, use this daily activity as a way to promote healing and health on an everyday (or every night) basis.

Why just care for your body when you can care for your mind and spirit at the very same time?

• **Have empathy**. Remember that you share your energy with the universal energy, as well as with the energy of all life on Earth.

Honor that energy by having empathy for all creatures great and small. Honor that energy by spreading kindness and peace, not cruelty or distress.

My grandfather was an avid fisherman and I spent much of my youth with him and my grandmother at their cabin on a lake in northern Manitoba.

I remember staying there after I returned from my trip to Italy in 1989. I was having a cup of coffee in the porch when I noticed my grandfather, who had returned from a fishing trip, had hung his catch up on a tree by the lake.

The fish were hanging from hooks in their mouths. Their bodies were shining in the afternoon sun, flopping feebly against the tree as the last of their life slipped away.

I couldn't stop myself. I put down my coffee cup, marched to the tree, and released each fish into the lake.

It was something I had done many times as a child; however, by leaving the fish on the tree, my grandfather had obviously assumed I had outgrown the practice. I hadn't. I couldn't.

Of course, he was furious. Furious, but resigned. His grand-daughter was a bleeding heart and there was really nothing to be done about it. Dinner was swimming away.

Yet I'll never forget the sight of those silvery bodies slipping away under the ripples of water, darting off into the depths like sparks of silver light to live another day.

I'll never forget the feeling. I felt what they felt. The wonder and joy of life and the desire of all living things to cling to it.

To this day, every time I'm in the grocery store and see a dead fish lying on a Styrofoam platter, its silvery body sealed to the plastic plate, I think of those fish.

Choose empathy. Choose life. Choose kindness. Choose to respect the energy of all life, for it is the same energy that animates your life. When you harm another living creature, you are harming a child of the same universe as you.

- **Laugh**. As I've said earlier, we live in an increasingly angry and sanctimonious world. Learn to laugh at it.

Laughter does the same thing as exercise – it floods the body and mind with feel-good endorphins. Choose, every single day, to have an easygoing spirit. Doing so will open up your body, mind and spirit to receive your intuitive self.

Remember the words of the ancient Greek philosopher Heraclitus: Humanius est deridere vitam quam deplorare (it is better to laugh at life than to cry over it).

• **Get outside.** Chances are good that you spend a great deal of time indoors. It's the world we live in. Whether you work in an office, hospital, school or you're a stay-at-home parent, you probably find yourself inside a lot. Most of our day to day business happens inside a building of some sort.

So get out! Eat your lunch outdoors. Take your kids swimming or sledding. Take the dog for more walks. Plant a garden or build a backyard fire-pit.

Even if it's cold outside, there's nothing stopping you from sticking your head out the door during your daily micro-break and take a deep breath of fresh air. It isn't just your body that needs it – your mind and spirit do, too.

• **Listen to music.** Music has a remarkable ability to "move" us in many ways. Physically, we feel more energetic. That's why many of us listen to music when we're working out, cleaning the house or car, or performing some other kind of physical task.

But music also moves us mentally, emotionally and spiritually. In that way, it can be used to stimulate right-brain activity and open up those areas of our mind that are responsible for accessing and processing intuition.

If you don't typically listen to a lot of music in your life, start doing so. If you already listen to music, challenge yourself to start listening to different styles.

One of my favorite things to do is to listen to music at night, while I'm driving. I don't know about you, but every now and then when I'm highway driving at night I slip into a strange type of reverie.

The black sky with the stars visible through my sunroof. The wash of white light from the headlights on the black road, illuminating my path as my car charges through the darkness. The looming shadows of trees along both sides of the road.

My own thoughts -- the ones I don't have the time to indulge during the day -- swirling in my mind. All of these things combine to create an aura that borders on the spiritual.

Add music to this mix, and your right-brain is firing on all cylinders. You're opening your mind to your intuitive self.

Every now and then, treat yourself to a solo night-drive. Listen to music – loudly! – and vary the style.

When I'm night driving, I like to listen to a range of artists, from Classical to Creedence Clearwater Revival. Sometimes I'll listen to my husband's selection, the ultimate in music eclecticism: everything from symphonic Awolnation to Aqua eurodance. I sing along at 120 km/h, under the stars.

By the time I pull back into my driveway, I feel like I've spent a month at the spa. I feel relaxed, open and receptive to my intuitive self.

Give it a try. Not only is it reinvigorating alone time, it has an intuition-enhancing purpose.

• **Face your fears**. Too many people let fear hold them hostage in life: you will never access your intuition while you are living in fear. You must face and overcome your fear(s).

I often work with people, both women and men, who are letting fear hold them hostage. This fear prevents them from accessing their intuitive selves.

The twenty-eight year old man who won't tell his wife to leave her extra-marital lover for fear she will leave him instead. The fifty-five year old woman with the unloving husband who won't ask more from him for fear of being alone "at her age."

If we let it, fear will make many decisions for us. The decision to attend a local college when what we really dream of is walking the halls of that big city university. The decision to stay in a job we hate instead of making a change or following a calling.

The decision to buy that new cookie-cutter house because the realtor says it's more salable than the character home we fell in love with. The decision to ignore that cutie beside us on the train because striking up a conversation would seem weird.

To make matters worse, fear often teams up with a twisted type of rationality. Unmarried middle-aged women never find happiness, right? A boring job is better than a risky one, right?

A new house is better than an old one, right? A local college is safer than a faraway university, right? People who strike up conversations with strangers on a train are weird, right? Why risk it. Maintain the status quo.

When we think like this, our fear convinces us that happiness is unachievable or irrelevant. Fear bullies us into believing that taking a risk, making that change, is too dangerous. We're safer "settling." This type of fear effectively gags our little voice and stifles our intuition.

To be clear, I'm not talking about healthy fear here: it's wise to fear things like financial debt and grizzly bears. I'm talking about the kind of fear that hijacks our decision-making and ignores our intuition, and that tends to hold us back in life rather than encouraging us to move forward.

Unhealthy fear-based decisions are the opposite of intuition-based decisions. Yet sadly, the voice of fear is often louder than the little voice of intuition. And as if that isn't bad enough, fear always leaves something in its wake – regret.

You might buy that new house, but you'll always long for the creak of old hardwood under your feet. You might make a decent living at that boring job, but one day you'll wish you would've tried something more exciting.

You might manage to stay married, but one day you'll look back and regret the years and self-dignity you sacrificed for someone who treated you like something stuck to the bottom of their shoe and who refused to change their ways.

You might hold your tongue on that train, but one day you'll kick yourself for not speaking up.

So ask yourself: What do I fear? How is that fear gagging my little voice? How is that fear preventing me from accessing the ancient intuition the universe itself gave to me?

Face that fear. Stare it down like the lying jerk it is. See fear for what it really is: a scary mask that hides your intuitive self. Rip off the mask and burn it. Today's a new day.

• **Debate yourself.** Most of us are pretty set in our ways. We are more or less certain of our values and opinions about things, and for the most part that doesn't tend to change much as we go through life.

Unfortunately, this complacency doesn't challenge our thinking. It doesn't make our minds "work" very hard. It leads to a sedentary mental lifestyle.

Yet to access the intuitive part of your brain, you will need your mind to be fit! Your mind must be willing and able to open up and to process new ideas and concepts.

In law school, I was taught the skill to both see and argue an issue from both sides. That didn't mean I had to agree with both sides. I just needed to see the issue in a holistic way, regardless of which side I supported or was fighting for.

I want you to start exercising that mental skill: the skill to see an issue in a holistic way. To see both sides, even the side you don't agree with, and to work through it in a rational way.

The issue you choose could be almost anything. It could be something as controversial as gun control or as trivial as a movie review.

The goal is to kick-start your brain so that both sides – the logical left and the intuitive right – are working at their full capacity.

- **Breathe**. I remember taking a fitness class once when the instructor shouted out, "Don't forget to breathe!"

What an idiot, I thought. How could I possibly forget to breathe? But then I realized I wasn't breathing. I was so focused on physically moving that I was holding my breath. Once I started breathing again, once that oxygen began to flood my body and brain, I felt stronger and I did better.

So…don't forget to breathe! In deeply and out slowly. Focus the breath of your life and learn to master it.

Learn to soothe yourself. Learn to control your own energy through focused breathing. Learn to use your own energy to welcome oxygen into your body and to stimulate your mind, especially the intuitive side of your brain.

- **Lights out**. In antiquity, homes and lives were lit by the warm glow of a fireplace or candlelight. Now, our homes and lives are lit by incandescent bulbs and the obnoxious glare of computer screens. While I'm the first one to applaud technology, I also think it can sometimes be soulless.

Once night a week, make the commitment to illuminate your home with only candlelight. Let the flickering flame of a beeswax candle fill your home with its soft amber glow, its crackling sound and its ancient heat energy.

Notice how different your home seems in this light. Notice the shadows cast on the walls. Notice how peaceful you feel.

Think about Firestarter's ancient fire. Think about the sacred fire that burned in Vesta's temple. Notice how these thoughts and this experience awakens in you a sense of your ancient self. Your intuition is in there! Illuminate it.

- **Embrace the seagull principle: expect this to work**. The truth is, we usually get out of life what we expect to get out of life.

People who expect to be treated well usually end up being treated well. People who expect happiness and fulfilment usually end up feeling happy and fulfilled.

At the same time, people who expect to be treated poorly usually end up being treated poorly. People who expect misery and disappointment usually end up feeling miserable and disappointed.

A long time ago, I remember seeing a poster of a white seagull flying against a blue sky. The caption read, "He can because he thinks he can."

That is, he *expects* to be able to fly. He has the expectation that when he flaps his wings he will stay up. He's a bird so it's a reasonable expectation. But you get the idea.

I encourage you to embrace the seagull principle in your life. Expect your intuition to work. Don't go down this path in a skeptical or experimental way.

Expect it to work.

Expect your intuition to work in the same way that you expect your arm to work when you reach for a cup of coffee. Expect your intuition to work in the same way that you expect your voice to work when you answer the telephone.

- **Reach into the past.** This book and this endeavour are all about reaching into the past. The deep, distant past. They're about reaching back into the ancient universe and into your ancient intuitive self. Like I said in the foreword, this book is a little time machine in your hands.

Right now, however, I want you to think about a past that isn't quite so ancient – the past years of your present life.

I want you to travel back in time. Back before the many and often competing obligations, demands and stressors of your life arose. Back to a time when your time was your own! When you get there, take a snapshot.

Now I want you to travel forward in time, back to the present day. Take another snapshot.

Compare the two snapshots. Mentally set them on the table, side by side, and take a good, long look at them.

What were you doing in the past snapshot? How does that compare to what you're doing in the present snapshot? Are there interests, passions or hobbies that you've let go over the years?

A happy, well-balanced person is going to find it much easier to tap into their intuition than an unhappy, unbalanced person. You know this is true. You know how essential it is that you reclaim some of your past interests or passions and make them a part of your everyday life.

Of course, this can't happen like it used to. You may not be able to spend as much time, money or energy on past interests. That doesn't mean you can't ignite a spark of them in your current life. Don't make excuses. Find a way to do it.

- **Be grateful for your life**. The ancient Roman orator Cicero has some words of wisdom about gratitude:

"Gratitude is not only the greatest of virtues, but the parent of all other virtues."

Be grateful for your life. As you awaken the ancient intuitive knowledge within you, that seed of knowledge the infinite universe planted inside you, be grateful for the gift.

One of my favorite movie scenes of all time is from a charming little cult film called *Joe Versus the Volcano*. To make a long story short, Joe (played by Tom Hanks) finds himself lost at sea for days on end, floating on some luggage he has managed to fasten together.

He is dehydrated and near death when, in the middle of a pitch black night, the moon rises as a colossal white disk above him. It is so big that it fills half the movie screen.

Despite being a breath away from dying – and knowing it – the sight stirs in him a sense of reverence for the universe.

He collapses to his knees and mutters, "Dear god, whose name I do not know, thank you for my life…I forgot how *big*. Thank you. Thank you for my life."

Strive to have that kind of gratitude, every day, for your life. It is bigger than you know. But with work and with gratitude, the universe will show you just how big it really is.

- **Vibrational energy**. The universal energy – of which your energy forms part of – is always in motion. It is always moving and vibrating – heat, light, sound, all of it.

As you access your ancient intuition, you are learning to "tune in" to the frequency of this energy.

I have found that listening to vibrational sound recordings has helped me, and many others, access our intuition.

Vibrational sound recordings are widely available in online and brick-and-mortar wellness shops. There are also many available for free on the Internet.

Vibrational sound recordings can produce intense feelings of relaxation, focus, healing and well-being.

They are sometimes called "brainwave music" or "healing tones," and when you listen to them you will understand why. They stimulate the right side of the brain, and can help awaken intuitive awareness and abilities.

In addition to vibrational sound recordings, you may wish to try a "singing bowl."

While these come in all shapes and sizes, the most practical type sits comfortably in one palm. The user then taps the rim of the bowl with a small wooden mallet, which causes the bowl to vibrate.

As it does, the user moves the mallet around the rim of the bowl, creating a distinct vibrational singing sound.

I have a singing bowl on my lararium. I find it works wonders, especially when I want to summon my intuition: it responds very well to a little vibrational serenading.

Like vibrational sound recordings, singing bowls are widely available in wellness shops, both online and traditional. I've also seen them in rock and gem shops, artisan shops, and spirituality shops.

Some have lovely designs; however, you may wish to find an unadorned one and paint it yourself, thus utilizing your creativity and fashioning a look that has special meaning to you.

• **Get creative**. We know that intuitive abilities are concentrated in the right side of the brain. So let's get that part of the brain going as much as we can! Create something. Anything. Take a pottery class or start finger-painting. Write a story, poem or song. Paint that singing bowl you just found. Exercise your creative mind.

Because I'm more of a left-brainer, I have to diligently work to keep my intuition burning in my right brain. One way I do this is through adult coloring. Yes, you heard me correctly. Adult coloring. And it's all the rage.

In a logic-based, stressed-out world like ours, adult coloring books are flying off the shelves as people intuitively recognize their need to unplug, power down and simply lose themselves in the creative process for a few minutes each day. I try to sit by either my fireplace or my Flamma candle, with a glass of wine in hand, and color for a few minutes every night.

If you're pressed for time and aren't a naturally creative person, give this a try. Some adult coloring books are absolutely gorgeous, with beautiful designs.

A friend of mine has one that features flowers. Every time she is finished a sheet, she glues it onto the wall in her sunroom: these now cover one wall like wallpaper. The effect is really stunning and beautifully unique. And best of all, her creative self is reflected back at her each time she looks at it.

- **Absorb celestial light: stargazing**. This is actually a nightly practice, but it's one that you should do regularly to stay connected to the universe and to stay mindful of the spark of ancient intuition already within you.

Take a moment and go back to look at the symbol under this heading: it sort of looks like a V sitting in a vessel with some kind of flame coming out of it.

That's because it *is* a V sitting in a vessel with a flame coming out of it! This is the planetary symbol for the asteroid called Vesta. The "V" is for Vesta, and it burns within the sacred hearth. A flame from the eternal fire flickers above it.

From ancient times, and continuing today, it is conventional for astronomers and scientists to name planets, asteroids and other celestial bodies after the Roman gods, goddesses and legendary figures.

This is done as a testament to the time when human curiosity, intelligence and intuition were at their best and brightest. See? The gods and goddesses do live on, and their names are as eternal as the universe itself. Cool stuff.

Every evening before you go to bed, take a moment to gaze up into the night sky. If you're lucky enough to live in an area where the stars can be easily seen, spend a moment in silent gratitude and reverence for your life.

If you don't live in an area where the stars can be easily seen, take a drive out of the city now and then to stargaze.

As you look up and lose yourself into the starry sky above, remember that you are actually looking into antiquity. You are looking into the ancient universe.

You're also looking into your ancient self.

After all, you are made of the same stuff as those twinkling stars above. You are made of the same energy that bounces off that big moon and those silver points of light.

You are looking at the same stars that Firestarter and her grouped looked at, and you are feeling the same sense of intuitive reverence that they felt.

• **Daily light reflection.** (*This candlelit practice has two parts: the first is a daily ritual presented here, while the second is a periodic and deeper ritual presented in the following section.*)

Light reflection is a daily ritual that consists of focusing on the Flamma of a beeswax candle. Its purpose is to spark the ancient intuitive awareness within you.

This ritual should be performed in a quiet room that can be made completely dark. You should be able to sit comfortably in this space, whether in a chair or on a floor cushion. You should also have a table or other stable surface upon which to burn your pure beeswax candle.

Enter this room and light your candle. Turn off the artificial lights in the room and sit in front of the candle.

Look into the flame. Watch its movements, study its orange color, and absorb its amber glow. Listen to it crackle as it burns the wood wick. Inhale its sweet fragrance.

Focus on these sensory inputs – the sight, sound and scent of the sacred, eternal flame – and push every other sight, sound, scent, taste and feeling from your mind and body.

As you sit before the Flamma, reflect upon what makes you happy or content. Reflect upon what is good about your life. Reflect upon what brings laughter and joy to your life.

Reflect upon your place in the ancient universe, and your journey to find your intuitive self. Reflect on the heat energy of the flame and how you are a part of it.

Stay focused and remain in a state of meditative reflection. Do not let your thoughts wander or "form" into specific questions or ideas.

Simply reflect on the flame and its sensory stimuli, and on your feelings of joy or well-being.

This ritual should be performed twice a day – morning and evening – so that you can focus your first and last thoughts and emotions of the day into affirming and positive ones. It should take five to fifteen minutes.

If you wish, you may pass a salted-flour wafer over the flame of your candle, or make an offering or libation to the flame, before you extinguish it.

This symbolically nourishes the flame of your intuition and pays tribute to the intuitive powers that fire can ignite within us. It is an ancient ritual that is still relevant today.

Beginning your day with this kind of light reflection can profoundly affect how your day is going to play out.

It can influence the way you speak to and treat others, the way you carry yourself, the way you react to unexpected or unpleasant events, the way you feel and the way others feel about you. Its effects can last all day long.

Best of all, it puts you in the state of mind, body and spirit that is most likely to summon and support your intuitive abilities.

By focusing on the flame's sensory stimuli – the sight, sound and scent of the sacred, eternal flame – you stimulate your own senses, including your sense of intuition.

Ending your day with this light reflection ritual reminds you to embrace the evening with joy, gratitude and perspective.

It also ensures that the last thoughts in your mind before you go to bed, and the last emotions in your heart, are those that can summon your intuition as you sleep.

This is very important, as intuitive dreaming is part of igniting your ancient intuition.

Light Reflection & Renewal: A Deeper Practice

The purpose of the daily practices and principles in the previous section is to get you into the general state of mind, body and spirit that will help you tap into your intuition. This endeavor is a holistic one that requires all aspects of your life to be balanced and thus open to receive intuitive messages.

Some of these practices and principles – such as the one about facing your fears – have a deeper purpose. They strive to "cleanse" your mind, body and spirit so that your intuition has a clean slate, so to speak, upon which to work.

They strive to remove distracting or destructive thoughts, memories, feelings, habits, behaviors and ideas that can put up a barrier between you and your intuitive self.

The practice presented here – light reflection and renewal – is a somewhat more in-depth ritual that also strives to remove such barriers. It is a type of guided-meditation ritual that I first presented in *The Vesta Secret*; however, I have received such wonderful feedback about it that I have chosen to include it here as well.

This purifying practice has its roots in a very old legend about two wolves, one you may have already heard. One evening, an old grandfather was talking to his grandson about a battle that goes on inside every person, every day.

He said, "The battle is between two wolves. One wolf is anger, jealousy, regret, hatred, unhappiness, resentment, ego, self-pity and self-doubt. The other wolf is serenity, gratitude, perspective, love, joy, empathy, humor, kindness and conviction."

The grandson asks, "Which wolf will win the battle?"

And the grandfather answers, "The one you feed."

This light reflection and renewal practice should be done in the same dark room in which you practice light reflection, since it is a cathartic extension of that daily ritual; however, this one requires that you have a pen and two sheets of paper, as well as a surface to write upon.

You will need just enough light to write by: if your beeswax candle isn't bright enough, find a heavily shaded lamp or soft-light bulb to write by.

Also, take fire-safe precautions: have a fire-safe receptacle ready as well as a means to extinguish the flame/fire if necessary.

To begin, sit in the darkened room with only the sight and sound of the Flamma beeswax candle before you.

Slowly picture in your mind a wildfire raging through an old forest. Hear its roaring power and feel its searing heat. See its black smoke fill the sky as it consumes everything in its path. Yet even as the fire destroys, it purifies.

It burns away years of dead foliage and rotting wood, so that the diversity and abundance of life that had been waiting dormant under its weight, trapped in the dark, can once again feel the warmth of the sun and experience life anew. The seeds of flowers and berries that had been dormant for decades can germinate into colorful life.

Yet it is a painful experience. It is heart wrenching to see trees that have stood for so long burn away and fall to ash. It's terrifying. It's hard to accept it and let it happen. We have been conditioned to reach for a bucket of water to try and stop it. Even when it's all for the greater good, it can be an excruciating experience.

The fire rages for days. Plumes of black smoke rise to fill the air. The heat and the sound are overpowering.

But then it all starts to subside. The fire dies down and a warm mist of rain descends upon the ashes, cooling them. Out of the sterile silence, a few birds start to sing.

And then through the black-charred pillars of the few trees still standing, you see two wolves. One is black and one is white.

They are both looking at you with their grey eyes, grey like the ashes, and they're running toward you, fast and determined as though on the hunt.

You know you can't run. If you do, they'll only pursue and there's no way you can outrun them. So you stand and wait as they race toward you with their grey eyes and their breath that mixes with the mist of the rain.

You stand and wait as the sound of their heavy breath, the pounding of their paws on the scorched forest floor, reverberates around you and closes in.

They run, fast and hard, until they are so close you expect to feel their weight knock you over and their sharp white teeth sink into your neck. But instead they stop abruptly at your feet, causing clouds of ash to swirl around your head.

They look up at you, panting and expectant. You can feel their hot breath on your legs. You can hear the deep growl in their throats. But they don't move, don't attack. They're waiting for something. But for what?

They're waiting to see which one of them you will feed.

And you will feed one of them. Not with meat, but with words that you will speak aloud.

But first, you will silently write each of them a letter.

If necessary, turn on the soft light in your room and gather your writing supplies.

On one sheet of paper, write to the black wolf about all the things in your life that make you angry, jealous, regretful, hateful, unhappy, resentful, egocentric, self-pitying or self-doubting.

You can write about who hurt you as a child or as an adult. About those you miss. About how you feel lost or have doubts. About the mistakes you have made. You can write about unrequited love, spouses who betrayed you, personal or financial failures, parents or partners who let you down.

Write to the wolf and tell him how these feelings affect your life and your relationships. How they scare you, sadden you or hold you back. How they keep you from knowing your true, whole self.

On the other sheet of paper, write to the white wolf about all the things in your life that make you serene, grateful, full of perspective, loving, joyful, empathetic, kind, make you laugh or give you conviction.

You can write about who has been kind to you. About your family and friendships and those who love you. About the good decisions you have made, what you cherish and how strong you can be. About your dreams for the future.

Write to the wolf and tell him how these feelings affect your life and your relationships. How they fill you with hope and energy, and push you forward.

Now decide which wolf you are going to feed.

Burn the letter to the wolf you want to starve, letting the paper disintegrate in the cleansing flame of your candle (you'll need your fire-safe receptacle here). As the paper disappears, so too does the hurt on it.

Gather the cooled ashes. Bury them in the ground or release them in the wind. It doesn't matter.

Now feed the wolf you want to survive: the white wolf. Read your letter – the one about joy, hope and gratitude – to him, in front of the Flamma. Let him feast on your words and watch him grow stronger and wiser than the other wolf.

Read the letter to him as many times as you like and then store it away in a secret place so that whenever he needs nourishment, you can take it out and read it to him again.

This light reflection and renewal practice can be performed on an as-needed basis, whenever you find yourself struggling with negative thoughts, memories or emotions that are holding you back.

I especially recommend you perform it when you feel certain mental or emotional barriers, including painful memories and past hurts or mistakes, are standing between you and your intuitive self.

Burn them away. Let the ancient power of fire reduce them to ashes while it renews and purifies your mind and spirit. Only then can your intuition grow to its full potential.

I love the power of this practice. I also love the wolf imagery. Do you remember the story of Romulus, founder of Rome? He was the one whose intuitive voice told him to build a sacred fire in the heart of Rome. The Temple of Vesta was eventually built around this fire to keep it eternally alight.

Well, it was a she-wolf who saved Romulus's life when he was stolen as an infant from his mother and left to die in the forest. A she-wolf nursed and nurtured him. As such, the ancient Romans saw the wolf as a symbol and source of strength, devotion and sacred intuitive awareness.

PART IV:

FIVE STEPS TO

IGNITE THE SPARK OF

ANCIENT AWARENESS

ALREADY WITHIN YOU

YOUR CIRCLE OF STONES

Fire burns in a circle. Not naturally, of course. Naturally, fire burns whichever way the wind is blowing or in whichever direction it finds material to consume.

But *we* burn fire in a circle – and come to think of it, we do that in a very natural way. An *intuitively* natural way. Firestarter intuitively knew it was natural and wise to arrange her stones in a circle around her sacred fire.

That intuitive knowledge continued and evolved as Romulus built his sacred fire within a circle of stones in the heart of what would grow to become the city of Rome.

His successors then build a circular hearth within which to burn this Flamma, embracing it as their eternal fire. The circular marble of the Temple of Vesta was then built around that.

The Vestal candle I received many years ago was circular, and so too are the new Flamma candles I create.

From Firestarter's time in pre-history to the Vestals' time in antiquity, and up to and including the modern digital age that we live in, we as humans intuitively build fire in a circle of some kind.

Have you ever seen a square campfire? Of course not. The first thing we do when we're camping (or lost in the woods!) is arrange stones in a circle and build a fire in the middle. By doing so, we claim that spot as a sort of "home." It becomes our focus and we are naturally drawn to it.

In fact, the earliest hut-homes of many ancient cultures, including the ancient Romans, were circular in shape.

Like fire – that symbol of eternity, the soul and intuitive knowledge – a circle is also symbolic. We talk about the circle of life, that eternal cycle that encompasses us all and that is animated by that same universal energy that animates us all.

We see the sun, the source of all life on our planet, as a life-giving circle of light and warmth. It is made of the same "star stuff" as we are made of. It lives and burns with the same universal energy that we live and burn with.

We see the moon, that silvery disk of reflective light in the night sky, as a symbol of reflection, clarity and brilliance. It inspires within us a certain poetry, and its breathtaking circle of changes – the lunar cycle – fills us with sacred wonder and celestial reassurance.

The five-step intuition-sparking process in this part of the book requires that you create an environment within which you can sit comfortably and perform each successive step. You can use the same space or room for this process that you use to perform the light reflection ritual and the deeper practice of light reflection and renewal in the previous section.

However, you may wish to add more symbolic power to this process by arranging a circle of stones around your Flamma or beeswax candle.

If you live by a river, you will find that river stones are ideal as they can be found in all sizes, from too-big-to-carry to fits-in-your-pocket. As a bonus, they are usually very smooth and offer a beautiful range of colors and patterns.

If you don't live by a river, take a walk and see what you can find on the ground in your area. Hiking trails or bike paths might offer some attractive stones for the taking.

You can also take a drive out of town, scanning the roadside for rocky offerings. Whether out of town or in town, stopping by a building project might yield some surprisingly unique finds as well, since the ground is dug up.

If you wish, you can purchase stones at an online or brick-and-mortar rock and gem shop. These can be pricey; however, choosing unpolished stones will save you money.

In fact, you can engage your creative right-brain intuitive abilities by polishing such stones yourself, thereby producing your own unique rocky works of art.

To do this, you will first need to wash your stones very well in soapy water. When they're dry, you will need to vigorously polish them with sandpaper (depending on size, you may want to use a hand-held or electric sander). When they're smooth, remove the grit by rinsing with water.

Finally, you will need powdered rock polish (available online and in and rock and gem shops) and a damp denim cloth. Scoop just a bit of the polish onto the cloth, and polish until your rocks look as shiny as you like. Wipe clean. Done!

To begin this five-step process, arrange your stones in a circle around your Flamma or beeswax candle.

You will also need the following:

- A box of wood matches to light your candle.
- At least one salted-flour wafer to nourish the Flamma and the flame of your own intuition: set this beside your candle.
- If you are seeking an intuitive answer to a specific question in your life, write the question on a piece of paper and set it near your candle. If you are seeking intuitive insight about a general area or issue in your life, write that down.

STEP ONE:
INTERNAL ILLUMINATION

Sit comfortably in front of your Flamma or beeswax candle: you should be within arm's reach of it as well as the other materials you will need (specifically, the wood matches and salted-flour wafer).

In order to illuminate and then ignite your intuitive self, you will first need to remove the barrier of your physical, mental and emotional self.

This means putting yourself into a deep state of relaxation. Bodily distractions, as well as distracting thoughts and feelings, will prevent you from focusing your energy where you need it to be.

- **Breathe** in deeply through your nose and hold your breath for a few moments before slowly exhaling through your mouth.

Repeat two or three more times, breathing in and out more slowly each time. Be aware of your breath and notice how it moves your body. Allow your breathing to return to normal.

- Tighten your **leg muscles, from your toes to your hips.** Hold the tension and feel your muscles warming. Now release the tension, letting your muscles feel relaxed and loose. Repeat one or two more times.

- Tighten the **muscles of your buttocks and back.** Hold the tension and feel your muscles warming. Now release the tension, letting your muscles feel relaxed and loose. Repeat one or two more times.

- Tighten your **arm muscles, from your fingertips to your shoulders.** Hold the tension and feel your muscles warming. Now release the tension, letting your muscles feel relaxed and loose. Repeat one or two more times.
- Tighten the **muscles of your stomach, chest, neck and face.** Hold the tension and feel your muscles warming. Now release the tension, letting your muscles feel relaxed and loose. Repeat one or two more times.
- Return to your **breathing**. Concentrate on creating a slow, regular breathing pattern. Visualize the warm air of the space around you entering your body, circulating within it, and then exiting.

This step relaxes both body and mind; however, you can help remove any stubborn distracting thoughts and emotions by consciously **removing the energy** you are directing toward them.

Visualize this energy as the amber light of your candle's flame, and picture it simply flying away from your mental and emotional functioning.

This visualization shifts your focus away from the distracting thoughts or feeling and onto the underlying energy you are expending for them.

That's good, because it is this energy that you will be using as you move through the subsequent steps in this process.

As you transition to step two, be sure to visualize this **amber light energy** both warming and **illuminating your being** from the inside out.

STEP TWO:
THE SENSORY BURN

This step builds on the previous step by moving you even deeper into the amber light energy that you now imagine is warmly illuminating your being from within.

At this point, you will consciously turn all of your focus onto the sight, sound and scent of the beeswax candle burning in front of you.

Let your **eyes absorb the amber glow** of the flickering flame.

Let your **ears absorb the crackle of fire** on the wood wick.

Let your **nostrils absorb the sweet fragrance** of the beeswax, deeply inhaling it and letting its vapor stimulate your pituitary gland and ignite the intuitive parts of your mind.

Breathe and simply *be*.

Breathe and exist only in this moment.

Take as much time as you need.

Open your senses, all of them, to the sight, sound and scent of the burning candle. Know that your senses are the gateway to your inner intuitive self.

As you transition to step three, be sure to visualize this gateway opening to allow the sensory energy of the candle to pass through.

STEP THREE:
INTUITIVE FUSION

Slowly lift your arms and place your hands, palms down, over the flame of your candle: place them just low enough to feel the heat energy of the candle's flame radiate into your palms.

You will be using the flame – the Flamma – as a focused source of energy. The flame will be to you what the Sun is to the Earth.

Spend some time **passively** accepting the flame's heat energy into your palms, feeling it fill your hands and fingers.

Now, more **consciously** draw the heat energy of the candle's flame into your palms, channeling it up along your arms, into your shoulders and up to your face.

Consciously draw this heat energy down your chest, into your stomach and down your legs to your feet.

Feel the heat energy of the flame **fuse** with the heat energy of your body. Feel the universal energy **fuse** with your personal energy.

Just as the universe uses the process of fusion to power the billions of stars that illuminate its darkest corners, so too will you use this process of fusion to illuminate your darkest corners.

Allow this fusion to ignite the spark of ancient intuition that lies deep within your being.

As you transition to step four, visualize your intuition as an eternal flame burning within the sacred hearth of your mind. Focus on it (the word hearth means focus in Latin).

STEP FOUR:
GUIDANCE & RECEPTION

If you are seeking an intuitive answer to a specific question, or looking for insight into a general issue or area, you can now begin to gently **guide your mindfulness** to the piece of paper lying near your candle (the one upon which you have previously written this question or issue).

While remaining in a state of intuitive fusion – with your palms held comfortably above the flame as described in step three – actively visualize the Flamma consuming the paper upon which this question or issue is written.

If you do not have a specific question or issue in mind, simply remain in a passive state of intuitive fusion with your hands held comfortably above the flame.

Rest and breathe as your intuition **receives** the stimulus of the question or issue. Rest and breathe as your intuition **receives** the stimulus of your presence and openness.

Keep all your senses open (as in step two) before your Flamma candle. As you look into the amber glow of your candle, as you hear the crackle of the wood wick, as you smell the sweet fragrance of the burning beeswax, open your body, mind and spirit to **receiving a message** from your intuition.

You may receive this message in various forms. You may hear it as a sentence, as words, as a poem or a song. You may feel it as an emotion or a physical sensation. You may see it as an image. You may sense it as a memory. You may conceptualize it as a thought or idea. Or you may *just know* it.

As you transition to step five, allow this intuitive message to fuse with your conscious mind.

STEP FIVE:
INTUITIVE EXPANSION

Once you have consciously received the message your intuition has sent, look into the flame of your candle and visualize it expanding into a larger point of light.

As you do, begin to slowly **expand your conscious awareness** of this message by processing it mentally, emotionally and physically. Consider the organic thoughts and feelings this message stirs in you.

To transition out of this five-step process, look into the flame of your candle and imagine it is the Sun. Now expand the visualization by drawing back until you can imagine the planets – Mercury, Venus, Earth, Mars, Jupiter, Saturn, Uranus, Neptune – orbiting around this amber point of light.

Expand the visualization and draw back even further, zooming out of our solar system, beyond the Milky Way galaxy and into the blackness of the larger universe.

Expand the visualization and draw back even further, moving past countless other suns, planets, comets, galaxies, cloudy nebulas, black holes and supernovas.

As you feel the heat energy of your candle against you palms, remember that its energy, and your energy, are part of the universal energy. When you journey into the expanded universe, you are journeying into your expanded self – specifically, your intuitive self.

To end this five-step process, take a few grounding breaths and zoom in your focus back to the flame. Pass a salted-flour wafer over it to symbolically nourish the flame of your intuitive self. Now extinguish your candle.

KEEPING THE EMBERS ALIGHT

As you can see, this five-step process is quite concise. It has to be. It requires such focused energy that a more complex process would defeat the purpose. Accessing and mastering your intuition is about seeing things simply and clearly, not mucking about in labyrinthine techniques.

Although this process is where it all comes together, the real work is done every day as you implement intuition-enhancing practices and principles into your daily life.

The five steps in this section simply bring structure and process to a holistic way of living, so that you can guide your intuitive mind to certain questions or areas, and so that you can receive the information it wants to give you.

Even after you extinguish your beeswax candle, you can keep the embers of your ancient intuition alight by reviewing this book – cover to cover – every now and then. Remember it in a holistic way, rather than just remembering these last pages.

(You can do it right now if you wish: quickly flip through the pages and then meet me back **HERE.**)

Travel back in time to the people, places and philosophies we have met along the way. Back to pre-history and Firestarter, and to the thunderbolt that changed her world.

Back to her daughters, to the chief hunter and the rest of the group, and to the way they were the first hominids to revere the sacred nature of fire, and to build ritual and religion around it.

Back to proto-history and Prometheus, and to his gift of fire and intuition. Back to the Classical Age and the Greek masters of philosophy, including Plato and Aristotle. Back to Pythagoras and the intuitive ability to fuse the abstract with the actual, the metaphysical with the physical.

Back to Romulus and the sacred hearth fire he started in the center of ancient Rome, and to the Temple of Vesta that ultimately encircled and embraced this eternal flame. Back to the Vestals who devoted their lives to the Flamma, and to the millions of people who honored it century after century.

Back to the Dark Ages when the flame of intuition was extinguished, only to be re-ignited and renewed – brighter than ever – in the Renaissance.

And right up to scientists in the Modern Age, from Albert Einstein to Carl Sagan, who recognized the intuitive mind as a sacred gift. To those brilliant minds that first recognized we are made of star stuff, and that our life's energy is part of the universe's eternal energy. Each of us has a universe within, both literally and figuratively.

You'll also want to review intuitive concepts such as the message of coincidence, looking for meaning, mind over matter and how faith is a passionate intuition.

You'll want to recall the genealogical tree of humanity, and how we are connected, genetically and intuitively, to all life that has lived, is living or will live on Earth.

You'll want to listen to your heart and trust your gut.

Of course, you will also want to keep engaging in the daily practices and principles in Part III. Your intuition requires comprehensive care and fine-tuning. Practice makes perfect.

So practice and perfect the art of living a curious, creative and grateful life. Actively observe the world around you. Connect with its energy through vibrational sound recordings or singing bowls. Connect with its energy by stargazing and absorbing celestial light.

Place a personal shrine or lararium at the entrance to your home and set a beeswax candle in the center. Let its flame be a symbol of eternity, the soul, the universal energy and the ancient intuitive awareness within you.

The more you can holistically fuse your life with the philosophies, practices and principles in this book, the more you will be able to achieve intuitive fusion with the Flamma and master this five-step process.

Few people find that the "light goes on" the first time. The goal is to immerse yourself in this five-step process in a natural way, so that you can do it even without this book.

As we've learned, it's all a process. Fire is a process. So too is life. You're in the process of life. So you might as well get everything you can out of your life: body, mind and soul.

Igniting the spark of ancient intuition within you can illuminate all areas of your life. It can shine light on your relationships, your career, your finances, your health and well-being, your spirituality and your overall happiness.

It can answer the types of questions you've been asking all your life. Some are simple: *Should I get on this plane?* Others are complex: *What is my place in the universe?*

It can give you the life that you just know you were meant to live. An intuitive life is an amazing life. It's a fascinating life. It's a fulfilling life. It's a limitless life.

Now go and live yours.

Thank you for reading!
For more information, visit
FlammaVesta.com

Made in the USA
Middletown, DE
07 March 2019